Bruno Gerussi

BRUNO:
L O V E

IN THE
KITCHEN

Breakfast Muffins

BRUNO:

LOVE IN THE KITCHEN

A Culinary Tribute by Nancy Morrison

TERRA BELLA PUBLISHERS

CANADA INC.

Dedication

In celebration of the lives of our two mothers, Nona and Jessie, who, under such differing circumstances, gave us the same love of food and entertaining, love of family and friends.

And to Bruno.

❦ ❦ ❦

Photography Credits:

Cover – Bruno Gerussi by David Gray

Black and White – Nancy Morrison & Bruno Gerussi by Patrice Bilawka

Food Photos – Hartley Charach

Other Photos from the private collection of Nancy Morrison and Bruno Gerussi

Canadian Cataloguing in Publication Data

Morrison, Nancy, 1937 – Bruno--love in the kitchen

Includes index.
ISBN 1-896171-20-6

1. Cookery, Canadian. I. Gerussi, Bruno, 1928 – 1995.
    II. Title. TX715.6.M67 1996 641.5971 C96-910165-1

Terra Bella Publishers
10 - 2471 Marine Drive
West Vancouver, B.C. V7V 1L3

Printed in Hong Kong by Kings Time Industries Ltd.
Thank you, Peter Ng.

Typeset in West Vancouver by
Accutype Business Services, Christin P. Bux.

Terra Bella Publishers thanks Jerry Wu, Derek Millar, Tracy Houston, Pat Feindel, Lazer's Edge, Debbie Cragg.

Special thanks to Mike, Maxine, Taylor and Alex.

Opposite Page Photos:
Top: Picnic on the Oregon Coast
Middle: Bruno, Bill Rand's Villa near Montalcino, Italy
Bottom: Bruno Gerussi - Beachcombers *farewell party*

CONTENTS

INTRODUCTION

Bruno loved good food and wine. Cooking was a pleasure, a way to express love for family and friends. On first meeting, our mutual joy of food and entertaining, surrounding ourselves with friends and family, and the joy of preparation and serving of food was obvious, and it grew with the years.

Initially, our cooking styles were very different. Bruno's featured his Italian heritage, suspicion of authority and rules, and with a sense of adventure. Mine was the Anglo, organized, linear, follow-the-recipe style. Surprisingly, the two did not collide; they melded.

Bruno gave up his disparaging remarks about English cooking. There was from the start his generosity about my cooking. His influence on me was profound, something I never really told him. With Bruno around, it was impossible not to be more courageous and instinctive in the kitchen.

I gave up my reticence and timidity about cooking with olive oil and garlic, and tried, with limited success, to curb the cream sauces in favour of Bruno's healthier preference for more vegetables and salads.

Organization was the key to enjoying entertaining, so we looked for recipes that could be done in advance, or that took little time.

Bruno's fame as a cook was enhanced by his television series in the '70s, "Celebrity Cooks." Interviews invariably touched on his passion for food. Fans never ceased to talk to him about cooking. And so many, including me,

wanted him to do another cooking show to share his energy, his wonderful enthusiasm for food.

Bruno and I began to talk about doing a cookbook three or four years ago. It would be Bruno's cookbook, but he was impatient with details, and the thought of organizing the writing and having to collect and confirm the recipes did not appeal to him. That was to be my role. Bruno appreciated my organization; he just never wanted to be cursed with it.

We tossed ideas around, chose our favourite recipes, laughed over anecdotes to include, and wondered how best to honour our mothers and their cooking. Our concept was a very personal cookbook.

We met with Pam McColl, our publisher, about six weeks before Bruno's death. It was impossible not to like her, and we were impressed by the fact that she had pursued us for over a year.

Bruno's death on November 21, 1995, was devastating. I could not believe my partner and loved one of 24 years was gone. I gave no thought to the book. Later, friends and family began their gentle urgings. Do the book.

An outpouring of love and support followed Bruno's death. Often from unexpected sources. A colleague wrote,

"... He lived his life with passion... Allow your sorrow to complete its course... Keep a kind heart and warm thoughts of your long relationship with Bruno, but let his presence go - slowly - gently."

This book is part of that process.

P A S T A

NONA

Nona was a legend.

Bruno was the eldest of her three sons, the one who defied peer pressure, schooling and authorities of all kinds. But never Nona. It was no mystery why Bruno adored strong women.

Bruno related with pride the story of the young Teresina who came from Northern Italy just after World War I. She came alone, across Canada by train, speaking no English, on her way to join an older brother in Lethbridge whom she had not seen for many years.

Other Italian immigrants on the train, many male and older, were too timid to leave the train at the frequent stops to obtain sandwiches and other food and drink. The land, language and currency were too foreign, but not for Teresina. She took their orders, got off the train at stops all across the vast country, bought sandwiches and made change for her fellow passengers. They tipped her in gratitude. She arrived with more money at the end of trip than when she began.

In Lethbridge, she met Enrico Gerussi, a stonemason and bricklayer, who was also a talented musician. They were married, and had three sons, Bruno, Tony and Dino.

In later years, to everyone, she was "Nona," still with that independence and courage, and what Bruno called uncommon strength.

Patsy Berton, Nona Gerussi, Rico Gerussi, Bruno –
before Rico & Patsy's wedding

NONA'S PASTA SAUCE
Tina Gerussi

When Bruno made Pasta Sauce, the genesis was Nona. We had agreed the recipe for Pasta Sauce was a must for this book, but there was nothing in writing when Bruno died. And Nona had cooked from the soul, not from the written page. Tina to the rescue.

Bruno's daughter, Tina Gerussi, who has more than a touch of Nona in her, also cuts a mean swath in the kitchen.

Bring out the largest stock pot you have. This recipe makes enough for two or three meals, plus lots left over for freezing.

In a large skillet, brown the ground meat. Drain the fat off in a colander.

Brown the steak pieces in a skillet, and add to the colander with the ground meat.

Set the soup bones to one side.

The carrots are sliced lengthwise, then chopped. Sauté in olive oil the chopped peppers, onions, celery and carrots in the stock pot on medium high heat for approximately 5 minutes, or until soft. Before sautéeing the celery, remove the elbows. They are mostly fibre, without the flavour.

Add the meat to the vegetables in the pot.

Add the chopped tomatoes with juice, tomato paste, 8 cups of water, sugar and spices to the pot and stir.

Put the soup bones into the pot.

Peel the garlic, leave whole and pierce each clove with a toothpick. Drop into the pot. Simmer everything together over low heat for at least 3 to 4 hours. Nona would make hers in the morning and leave it to simmer all day. After 2 hours, remove each piece of garlic with a spoon. Remove the toothpick, and mash the garlic in the spoon with a fork. Return the mash to the pot and stir in.

During the last hour of cooking, add the sliced mushrooms and peas.

This sauce is almost like a stew, and can be used with any kind of pasta. Nona almost always served it with spaghetti. She would boil the pasta and return the pasta to the pot. At this point Dad would always add butter to the pasta, but Nona would just add a cup or two of the sauce (mostly the liquid) to keep the spaghetti from sticking. Then serve with additional sauce on top.

2 lbs. medium to lean ground beef
1 lb. ground veal
1 lb. round steak, cut into bite size pieces
2 or 3 marrow bones (soup bones)
Beef bouillon cubes or paste
1/4 cup olive oil
2 large carrots, chopped, approximately 1 cup
2 green peppers, chopped, approximately 2 cups
2 large onions, chopped, approximately 2 cups
1 bunch of celery (use top part of celery, using the leaves and partial stalks)
2 - 28 ounce cans of plum tomatoes, chopped, with juice
2 - 13 ounce cans of tomato paste
8 cups water (or to desired consistency)
1 tablespoon brown sugar
1 teaspoon salt
1 teaspoon oregano
1 teaspoon basil
1 teaspoon cinnamon
3/4 teaspoon ground pepper
3/4 teaspoon allspice
3/4 teaspoon marjoram
Pinch of thyme
1/8 teaspoon ground cloves
6 cloves of garlic
2 cups sliced mushrooms
1 cup fresh or frozen peas (optional)

R I S O T T A
& P O L E N T A

Nona also used this sauce when making her risotto, polenta and gnocchi. For the risotto, she would use chicken broth or water to cook the rice (adding a cup at a time while constantly stirring for about 1/2 hr.). During the last stages, she would add some sauce and freshly grated parmesan cheese (which we had to grate by hand upon walking in the door), then serve with more sauce on top.

The polenta she made was also boiled on the stove while constantly stirring and adding liquid as it is cooked. She would then butter and pour the polenta into a pie plate and let cool. As it cooled it would mold to the plate. She would then cut it into slices (sometimes removing the whole thing upside down onto a serving plate) and serve with the sauce on top.

The spaghetti was served with romano cheese, or fava beans, sliced onions with oil drizzled on top as a side dish. Sometimes cooked young tender dandelion greens or cooked radicchio (both from her garden) and bread heated in a brown paper bag sprinkled with water in a warm oven. And lots of home made wine. The gnocchi was served with sauce on top as well.

One of the rituals when arriving at Nona's around lunch or dinner time was going straight to the fridge, digging into the lower right hand crisper and bringing out the salami and cheese. She would buy her salami and cheese whole and we would have to slice it by hand. The trick was to slice the salami as thinly as you could (Dad and Tony were pros, with Dino a close second,) and keep up the supply enough to look like you were actually working, as everyone kept grabbing it from the cutting board and plate before it got to the table. There were usually 2 or 3 shift changes before dinner was served. We were stuck grating the cheese until we were deemed old enough to handle the knife.

Discrimination

Being Italian and poor as a school boy in New Westminster, during the years of World War II, was not an easy childhood.

As a boy, Bruno's family nicknamed him "Il Vecchio," the old one. He had learned to listen and discern at a young age. He would later say, "Philosophy is not what you say or what you think, it's what you do, how you discipline your life."

The discrimination Bruno experienced as a child left him with a passionate sense of justice, an innate respect and courtesy for those who work at the meanest of jobs. He had been there. At 14, still in school, he worked on the dangerous green chain in the pulp mill in New Westminster, where a mis-step could cost a hand or an arm.

In his late teens, Bruno spent three years in Seattle on a drama scholarship. To support himself, he washed dishes at a local restaurant every night, from 1:00 a.m. to 4:00 a.m.. He hated washing dishes.

Through his first-hand knowledge of the hospitality industry, he knew how little waiters and bartenders made. His tips were generous to a fault. It had nothing to do with celebrity, everything to do with respect. He never sent a dish back to the kitchen, no matter how awful the food. If asked why so little was eaten, he would smile and say, "Have to watch my weight." But never a complaint.

Bruno just never picked on the little guys.

N O N A ' S
G N O C C H I
Gino Gerussi

3 lbs. of gem or russet potatoes

3 cups flour

Peel and boil the potatoes until tender. Remove the potatoes from the water and mash.

Once the potatoes are mashed, add 3 cups of flour and knead into a dough. Make sure your surface is floured continuously and keep your hands floured or the gnocchi may become soggy.

Once the dough is done, cut off a chunk and roll into strips about 1" thick, then cut that strip into 1" pieces. Place each piece on a floured cloth making sure the gnocchi do not touch each other. Repeat with the rest of the dough.

In another pot, bring water to a boil on high heat and put the gnocchi in the water. As soon as the gnocchi float to the top, they are ready to be removed and put on a clean dry cloth.

Place the gnocchi in a casserole dish and stir in Nona's Sauce, about 3 cups. Sprinkle with Parmesan cheese and serve.

Or, put gnocchi in a casserole dish and coat with sauce and about 1/4 cup of butter and 1/2 cup of Parmesan cheese. Bake at 400 degrees F. for 5 to 10 minutes. Sprinkle with Parmesan cheese before serving. Serves 5 to 6 people.

Left to right, Kenny Neal, Bruno, Tina Gerussi, Rico Gerussi, Syreeta Neal, Liam Gerussi, Michaela Gerussi, Patsy Berton, Graeme Gerussi

Bruno's pride and joy – his family – on the dock of his cabin on Lake Simcoe, Ontario, with 5 grandchildren and Rico, Patsy and Tina.

Judy LaMarsh

It was September, 1972, and the Great LaMarsh was coming to Vancouver to do talk radio, head to head, mike to mike, with Jack Webster, King of the open lines. She with the "golden brown voice," said Webster, who color-coded voices, brown being best.

Judy, famous throughout Canada by her first name only, Canada's first female Minister of Health and Welfare, second only female cabinet minister in 1963, trial lawyer, politician, broadcaster, columnist and author. She was brilliant, funny, courageous, multi-lingual, honest, ethical, warm and one of the finest friends one could ever hope to have.

There had been more than a little hype about Judy presuming to take on Webster, and when she arrived late Sunday in Vancouver, Judy was horrified to find that nothing was set up for her first three hour radio show, due to begin at 9:05 the next morning. But she knew an old friend was nearby, one with the best voice, interview and entertainment skills in the country, Bruno. His CBC radio show, "Gerussi!," had revolutionized radio in the mid '60s, when Bruno, and his friend and producer, Diana Filer, brought together a remarkable and unsurpassed blend of politics, satire, poetry, humour, music and sheer entertainment never before heard on radio, the original upon which all subsequent CBC morning shows were patterned.

Bruno had left the radio show after several years to come to the West Coast to begin filming "Beachcombers" at Gibsons, and it was there Judy found him. Would he come and do the show with her that next morning? Of course.
The director agreed to shoot around him for half a day, and Bruno hired a water taxi early that Monday morning to get from Gibsons to Vancouver. Then two old friends had fun on the radio that first day of Judy's career as a broadcaster. Bruno was every inch a political junkie, as was Judy. They both devoured newspapers, magazines and books, although few could match Judy's reading. Their partisan

JUDY LaMARSH'S SPAGHETTI CARBONARA

Judy was a superb cook and hostess. Her grand-scale New Year's Eve dinner parties were feasts. There was a generosity in Judy, that same quality that so typified Bruno.

1 lb. spaghetti
3 eggs, beaten
1/3 cup grated Parmesan cheese
1/3 cup grated Romano cheese
6 slices bacon, sliced fine
2 tablespoons olive oil
1/3 cup dry white wine
Freshly ground black pepper

Cook the spaghetti in boiling, salted water for 7 or 8 minutes until a bit firm.

Have the eggs at room temperature. Beat together with the cheeses.

Fry the bacon in olive oil until crisp. Add the wine and cook until the wine evaporates.

Drain the spaghetti and return to the hot saucepan.

Add the egg and cheese mixture and the hot bacon-oil mixture and plenty of pepper.

Stir rapidly so the egg mixture cooks onto the hot spaghetti. Serve on hot plates.

politics might have been different, but their passions for politics and people, issues and justice, were the same.

My connection with Judy began in February, 1963. I was about to be called to the Bar in Ontario as a lawyer, and no one would hire me. Except my Dad, who would have welcomed me back to Saskatchewan to practise with him, but that would have meant I could not make it on my own, so I kept looking in Ontario. Those were the days when the guys just looked at you and said, "We don't hire girls." But that's another book.

Enter Judy, well known as an expert trial lawyer, extraordinary for a woman in those days, a backbencher in the House of Commons, and desperately looking for a junior for her law office in Niagara Falls. The day I joined her law office, fresh from my call to the Bar, was the day she was first appointed to the federal Cabinet as Minister of Health and Welfare, April 22, 1963. She could no longer practise law, so I became her office, and the only woman lawyer in three counties, Welland, Haldiman and Lincoln. I stayed for three and a half years, and Judy became my friend and mentor.

And much later she became our match-maker.

After Bruno did Judy's radio show that September in 1972, he invited her to come to Gibsons for Thanksgiving. She said she would, but only if she could bring a friend. And being a rascal and an eternal tease, Judy deliberately did not say whether the friend was male or female. Bruno wondered, but deliberately did not ask. Of course, he said, bring the friend.

Judy had forgotten I was out of town on a holiday. I returned late Friday night before the Thanksgiving weekend. The phone was ringing. "Where the hell have you been?" yelled LaMarsh. "We have to go to Gibsons tomorrow." "Why?" I asked. "Well, you always said you would give your left arm to meet Gerussi. We've been invited to his place for Thanksgiving." That was October 5, 1972.

Judy died at the impossibly young age of 55 in 1980 of pancreatic cancer. She was, like Bruno, the brightest of comets to streak across our heavens.

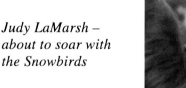 *Judy LaMarsh – about to soar with the Snowbirds*

Umberto

Umberto Menghi, Vancouver's famous restaurateur, has been a dear friend for many years. Umberto comes from a close and loving family who live near Pisa, Italy. They embraced Bruno as a son, visiting in Gibsons and Deep Cove, and hosting us in Italy.

Umberto's late mother, affectionately called Mamma Delia, was a younger version of Nona, an intuitive, marvellous cook, whose touch with food made you believe in magic.

Two Italian sons, blessed with extraordinary families, who inherited their mothers' love of cooking and ease of entertaining. Family, hearth, friends, food, wine and love.

*Top: Bruno and great
friend Umberto Menghi*

*Bottom: Bruno and Mamma Delia,
Umberto's Mother, Italy 1984*

A good chef always samples the food for taste, quality control, texture and presentation. Umberto took this to a higher plane one night.

Following theatre one evening, Bruno and I were having dinner at Umberto's original restaurant, "Umberto's," with Michael Learned, an old friend of Bruno's from Stratford days, and an actress perhaps best known for her role as the mother in "The Waltons." There were six of us seated at an oblong table, three on each side. The restaurant was full, noisy and happy, as Umberto's restaurants are. Just as our entrées were served, Umberto appeared, and glanced down at Bruno's plate of tortellini. Without a word, Umberto reached over, took Bruno's fork, speared a tortellini, and popped it into his mouth. As Umberto chewed reflectively, he reached over to spear another fork of tortellini, again into his mouth. More reflective chewing, then a quick motion to a nearby waiter for the pepper grinder. The pepper grinder was applied, and Umberto snaffled another two forkfuls of tortellini, nodding his head in slight approval by this time. Thirst overcame him, he reached for Bruno's full glass of red wine, and took a satisfying gulp or two.

He summoned more Parmesan. Our guests at the table were watching, transfixed, not realizing this was the owner of the restaurant, and an old friend.

In the midst of Umberto's increasingly enthusiastic sampling, he reached back, grabbed an empty chair, and pulled it up to the end of the table, having commandeered Bruno's napkin, utensils, plate and wine glass by this time. The rest of the restaurant was watching with fascination, and all Bruno could do was laugh, as his entire meal and wine disappeared before his eyes. By the time Umberto was finished, not a drop of wine or tortellini remained; the chef had enjoyed his meal immensely. Finished, Umberto wiped his mouth, stood up from the table and left, never once having uttered a word, other than the murmured approval of his own food, leaving Bruno helpless with laughter.

When Bruno's order arrived once more, it came with a bottle of wine, compliments of Umberto.

Eating Italian in Hawaii

As restaurant reviews go, it did not begin well.

"They should burn this place to the ground." Bruno always did have good instincts.

This was an alleged Italian restaurant in Princeville, on the north end of the Island of Kauai, Hawaii.

The Italian antipasto arrived, and did nothing to change the diagnosis, or prognosis.

Warm California wine had preceded it. "Weasel piss," he murmured. Not a good sign. One of his lower rankings for wine.

"Keep it covered," said the waitress, as she placed cocktail napkins over the half carafes of white and red wine. "The flies."

She was right.

The flies kept scrupulously away from the food.

Italy

We flew to Italy in late September, 1984, for a month in Tuscany. Midway over the Atlantic, the tall, handsome, lean Captain, right out of central casting and a Canadian Airlines ad, came to talk to Bruno. He was a fan. Especially of Bruno's cooking show, "Celebrity Cooks."

To the delight of any feminist heart, these two macho, take-no-prisoners men talked for an hour about the virtues of extra virgin olive oil, the danger of burning the garlic, and where and how to choose the finest salami. The Canucks, the Bulls and the Dodgers were never mentioned.

*Bruno and Nancy with members
of Umberto's family in
Pontedera, Italy, 1984*

PASTA WITH GARLIC AND OIL

For whatever reasons, Bruno had never cooked this for me before our trip to Italy. It was there I was introduced to the dish. We were in the beautiful walled, Tuscany town of San Gimignano. This is the town of the tall towers, or keeps, once numbering dozens, now only nine left standing, of differing sizes and shapes. It was dark by the time we reached San Gimignano, and our first glimpse was of a floodlit castle in the distance. Then the floodlit towers became visible, and we had found one of our favourite spots in Italy. It is located on top of a hill, of course. Tuscans always built on top of the big hills. And they built well. We circled our way around the outside walls into the heart of the town, where our hotel, La Cisterna, was located. It featured a terrace restaurant overlooking the town and the valley called Val d'Elsa.

Besides featuring some of the most beautiful pottery and ceramics in Tuscany, the town is also famous for a superior white wine, the Vernaccia de San Gimignano.

One leisurely lunch, while sampling some suitably chilled Vernaccia, Bruno ordered a dish whose name I couldn't understand. Spaghetti con aglio e olio. When I asked him what it was, he said it was spaghetti with garlic and oil. That sounded strange to these Anglo-Saxon taste buds. The dish arrived, and I reached over with my usual curious fork. It was wonderful. Bruno could not believe that I had never had it before.

From that point on, it became a favourite. It was a dish that Bruno had grown up with, and one that we used as an appetizer, a side dish, a late night snack, or the main course for a supper.

Heat the oil and butter in the wok, add the garlic and sauté gently until it is golden. Be sure not to burn the garlic. Set this to one side, but keep it warm.

Cook the pasta in a large pot of boiling water with salt and one tablespoon of olive oil added to the water. Cook the pasta about 5 to 7 minutes, or until al dente. Do not overcook. Drain the pasta well, and add the pasta to the garlic and oil. Mix thoroughly over a gentle heat for a minute or two. Season with freshly ground pepper and serve on warm plates.

Great with a simple green salad and a glass of wine.

2/3 cup extra virgin olive oil

2 tablespoons butter

3 tablespoons garlic, chopped fine

Ground pepper to taste

1 lb. pasta, spaghetti suggested

Use a large teflon wok to sauté the garlic.

Bruno and Bill Swope.
Semi-mystical ceremony of
opening wine preceding lunch
at Gibsons.

Bruno always referred to his mother with great admiration. "The old Mother Earth, the Lioness."

He talked about her extraordinary ability to make meals out of nothing.

Nona's magic in making wine remains legendary. Former NDP Cabinet Minister Dennis Cocke remembers, as a young man, drinking that extraordinary homemade red wine made by Nona.

Bruno's parents would get grapes from California, and Bruno and his brothers would stomp them. Bruno would laugh that his legs were purple until he was 15 years old.

After the grapes were crushed, they would be put in the barrel. Bruno told of Nona, lying on the chesterfield during the night, waiting for just the right moment, when she sensed that the temperature and the grapes were exactly right. Then she would rouse everyone out of their beds, and everyone got up immediately, regardless of the hour. His recalled that it was invariably in the middle of the night. But Nona knew just when to take the grapes out of the barrel.

On our trip to Italy in 1984, we stayed for two weeks in the historic villa owned by our friend, Bill Rand, at Montalcino and Bruno marvelled at the famous red wines, Brunello di Montalcino. He picked his favourite years, and brought back three or four cases to Canada. One of the cases mysteriously disappeared on the long and dangerous journey back through customs.

S E A F O O D

Bruno and seafood were a natural combination. He had a light touch, knowing exactly how long to cook fish.

He also knew who sold the freshest seafood. At Gibsons or Steveston, we could buy seafood right off the fish boats. Otherwise, our favourite was The Crab Shop on the way to Deep Cove in North Vancouver, where they catch and cook their famous Dungeness crab, and sell only the freshest from the ocean.

And Bruno and I gravitated to restaurants that cooked seafood simply and wonderfully. Like "The Savoury" in Deep Cove, our "local" for almost twenty years, an easy one-half block stroll from my first cottage, and a safe, no-driving, one-half block lurch home.

On our trip to Venice, the City of Islands that enchanted us, we had our most memorable restaurant meal in Italy, every course featuring seafood. It began with an early morning stroll from our hotel, the Gabrielli-Sandwirth on the Grand Canal, to St. Mark's Square through the mid-morning fog on a warm October day.

A huckster stopped us and insisted we take two "free" tickets for a water taxi to the Island of Murano, the century-old centre of the glass-making industry in Italy. We knew there was no such thing as a free ride, but off we went, past Cemetery Island, and on to Murano. We watched glass made in red hot furnaces, moulded, pressed and clipped by several apprentices and two masters, all of whom kept drinking cold glasses of beer to refresh their dehydrated bodies. We bought some wonderful crystal, as we knew we would.

As we were leaving the island, our host asked if we liked seafood. He was a large, good-natured man, who looked like he knew the business end of a fork. A ferryboat was just leaving for the Island of Burano, where there was an excellent restaurant featuring fish. Burano was a fishing village we should see. Our resistance to temptation was pleasantly low that day.

*Bruno on one of the canals
of Venice, heading for
the Island of Murano*

Burano was a miniature Venice, the buildings all painted in fresh and different colours, the canals and bridges scaled down versions of those in Venice. As an added surprise, we learned it was the centre and original home of Venice's lace industry.

Bruno's Taurus instincts took us unerringly up the right via to the restaurant, "Osteria Ai Pescatori," and oh, what a lunch we had. It began with antipasto pescatori, varieties of local seafood, followed by spaghetti co il pevorassoli, small tasty mussels, almost sweet, then scampi and two or three other dishes whose names escape, but not the memory of their taste. There were at least two bottles of cold wonderful white wine. Or was it three?

Nancy, Rome, 1984. A quiet Sunday morning paper over breakfast.

Opposite:

Bruno, Jacquie and David Sims cooking Umberto's prawns on a trip to the Napa Valley.

UMBERTO'S PRAWNS

*This is really Umberto's recipe, called "Gamberoni Affinocchiati," from his first cookbook, **The Umberto Menghi Cookbook**, published by Talonbooks in 1982. From the moment Umberto's cookbook came out, this recipe became one of Bruno's favourites. He introduced it to our friends in Saskatchewan when we made our annual summer trip to Crystal Lake, north of Yorkton. We would bring pounds of frozen prawns from Vancouver, and Bruno made sure we never forgot the Pernod.*

Sauté the prawns in butter over medium heat for just a minute or two, turning them at least once. Do not overcook.

Add the Pernod and reduce the heat somewhat, and simmer for a minute or two.

Add the cream and cook on medium heat until the cream just begins to bubble. Season with salt and pepper, add the lemon juice directly onto the prawns and stir quickly until blended.

Serve the prawns on a warm platter or warm plates, add the additional sauce, and sprinkle with parsley.

This is not a dish that you prepare ahead of time. It only takes a few minutes, and there is a minimum of mess in the kitchen. Prepare it then and there for your guests.

Thank you, Umberto, for years of pleasure with this recipe.

1 lb. prawns

2 tablespoons butter

2 tablespoons Pernod

1/2 cup whipping cream

Salt and freshly ground black pepper to taste

Juice of 1/2 lemon

1 teaspoon fresh parsley, finely chopped

SWEET PEPPER CRAB CAKES

1 pound crab meat
1/4 medium green pepper, chopped fine
1/2 red pepper, chopped fine
1/2 yellow pepper, chopped fine
3 tablespoons large Spanish onion, chopped fine
Pinch of cayenne
Pinch of sugar
1 teaspoon salt
2 eggs, slightly beaten
1 tablespoon parsley
1/2 teaspoon dry mustard
1 tablespoon tarragon
2 tablespoons heavy cream
1/2 cup cooked mashed potatoes
1/4 cup light bread crumbs
3 tablespoons butter
1 tablespoon olive oil
Flour to coat

Melt 2 tablespoons of butter in a skillet and sauté the onion and peppers over medium heat until cooked soft.

Add all the seasonings to the onion and peppers; then into a bowl place the potatoes, bread crumbs and the onion-and-pepper mixture with the seasonings, the slightly beaten eggs, the cream, and finally the crab meat. Add just enough cream to make the mixture hold together. Mix all together well.

Shape into large flat cakes. Coat each cake in flour. The least messy way is to place flour on a large sheet of wax paper and flip the cakes in the flour on it.

In a frying pan place butter and a small amount of olive oil. Fry each side of the crab cakes until brown.

Serve with papaya sauce, and pink pickled ginger on the side, thinly sliced.

PAPAYA SAUCE

1 papaya, seeds and skin removed
2 tablespoons fresh lemon juice
1/2 teaspoon powdered ginger

Combine in a food processor the papaya, fresh lemon juice, and powdered ginger. Mix well and serve as a sauce with the crab cakes.

This is a pale imitation of the crab cakes and sauce served by Peter Weiser of La Toque Blanche, a superb French restaurant in West Vancouver, another "local" into which we wandered with regularity.

SHEILA'S SEAFOOD CASSEROLE

One taste of this at my cousins, Don and Sheila Graham's, and we had to have the recipe.

1 lb. scallops, cut in half

1-1/2 lbs. shrimp, lightly cooked

6 tablespoons butter

1/3 cup flour

1/2 teaspoon salt

1/4 teaspoon nutmeg

1/4 teaspoon cayenne

1 cup milk

1 cup whipping cream

3 egg yolks

1/2 cup dry sherry

Sauté the scallops in butter until no longer transparent, just a few minutes. Do the same with the shrimp. Drain and set aside.

Make a white sauce by melting the butter, then adding the flour and the seasonings. Cook until bubbly and stir in the milk and the cream. Stir continuously until thick.

Remove from heat.

Beat egg yolks lightly, and add the sherry. Add one-half the cream sauce mixture to the sherry mixture. Then add that mixture back into the main white sauce mixture. Cook for 3 minutes on top of the stove.

Fold in the scallops and shrimp.

Place in a casserole dish and cook uncovered, at 250 degrees F for 1 hour or less.

Serve with white rice and snow peas, or fresh asparagus.

CAPE BRETON FISH CHOWDER

1 large piece fresh cod

2 potatoes, peeled and chopped fairly small (1/2 inch cubes)

1/2 sweet onion, peeled and chopped fine

Salt pork, chopped fine, or cooked bacon, chopped fine.

Lemon pepper to taste

1/4 to 1/2 teaspoon mace

2 cans condensed milk

Sauté the onions in a small amount of butter, adding a small amount of water to soften, and cook until transparent.

Cook the salt pork in a small amount of butter, and drain on paper towelling when cooked.

Cook the potatoes gently in water until done; drain, saving the water. Cut the cod into large bite size pieces and cook in the potato water until the fish has lost its transparency, just a few minutes. Drain and save the water.

Combine in a large saucepan the two tins of condensed milk, the potatoes, salt pork, onions and butter, a generous amount of lemon pepper, mace and the cooked cod. Warm over gentle heat. Do not bring to a boil.

If the chowder is too thick for your taste, it can be made thinner by adding some of the potato water you have saved.

GIBSONS BAKED SALMON

SALMON

Bruno believed salmon should be barbecued, and did so often with flair. He would wrap the salmon in heavy tinfoil, first putting in lemon slices, fresh dill, some slices of onion, salt and pepper and a bit of butter. But on one occasion he and another great barbecue chef, Hugh Lyons, blotted their barbecue copy books with their women, namely Sandra and me.

We were all at Crystal Lake, our summer haven, flushed from a game of golf and 19th hole liquid refreshments. The great ones, Bruno and Hugh, were on the patio, barbecuing and resolving the political problems of the day. In they came with blackened, dry, charcoal chunks of what had once been wild salmon lovingly brought from the West Coast.

So sometimes, we turned to Plan B for cooking salmon - baking it in the oven, and setting the timer.

In a large shallow baking pan, lay the salmon on a large sheet of heavy tinfoil that has been lightly oiled under the fish. This will prevent it from sticking after baking, making it easier to transfer the salmon onto the serving platter.

Place in the cavity of the salmon several stalks of fresh dill (or tarragon), several slices of lemon, salt and pepper and a dab of butter. Place the rest of the dill, lemon and butter on top of the salmon, and seal the tinfoil around and over the salmon - leaving some space inside for juices to collect during the cooking.

Bake in a 350 degree F oven for approximately 10 minutes per pound - or until the salmon flakes easily with a fork. Do not overcook.

1 whole salmon, 4 to 6 pounds

Several stalks of fresh dill
  (or tarragon)

2 lemons, sliced

Salt and pepper to taste

2 tablespoons butter (optional)

GRAVLAX

This takes a five day head start to prepare. Your guests know you love them when gravlax appears.

Mix together the salt, sugar and crushed pepper.

Have the salmon prepared as two long fillets, with the skin left on each side. In a long glass cakepan, spread fresh dill on the bottom, place one fillet, skin side down, then gently rub the combined salt, pepper and sugar onto the red flesh of the exposed fillet; lay a bed of fresh dill on top. Place the second fillet, which has also been rubbed with the salt, sugar and pepper, flesh down on top of the bed of dill; then spread the rest of the salt, sugar and pepper on top of the second fillet (on top of the outer skin of the salmon), and lay another bed of fresh dill.

Cover the pan tightly with heavy aluminum foil, and refrigerate for five days, weighted.

For weight, some use bricks. Bruno and I preferred full wine bottles, which need to be kept chilled anyway. Turn the salmon over every 12 hours, and baste with the juices that form.

Remove the salmon from the pan, throw away the dill, juices, and scrape the remaining peppercorns gently from the flesh. Squeeze some fresh lemon juice over the salmon. Gravlax will stay in the fridge for a week or two, or can be frozen, the same as smoked salmon.

To serve, slice the gravlax as thin as possible.

When you slice it, make sure it is cold, or even partly frozen, so that it slices more easily. Serve with rye or whole wheat bread and gravlax sauce.

1/2 cup white sugar

1/4 cup coarse salt

1/4 cup regular salt

1/4 cup white peppercorns, crushed

Fresh dill, a lot

1 salmon, filleted, with outer skin left on.

MARGARETA'S GRAVLAX SAUCE

When I first tried making gravlax years ago, I mentioned it to Margareta, famous for her West Coast clothing designs and women's wear stores. "And the sauce, of course," said Margareta. "What sauce?" So she hauled me back into her design studio and quickly rattled off the ingredients and procedure, some more-or-less measurements, and very firm instructions that we were not to serve the gravlax without the sauce. Margareta was right. Allan Fotheringham was in on that intitial tasting, and gave the gravlax and sauce its first press clipping.

---

2 tablespoons dry mustard

4 tablespoons sugar

2 tablespoons Dijon mustard

4 tablespoons sugar

4 tablespoons vinegar

3 cups Crisco oil

1 cup fresh dill, chopped fine

Combine the dry mustard with 3 or 4 tablespoons of sugar, and enough water to mix and stir. Add two tablespoons of Dijon mustard. Stir.

Add 4 more tablespoons white sugar, and 4 tablespoons of vinegar. (If this seems too bitter with mustard, add more sugar at this point.) Beat together, using a whisk.

Then slowly beat in the Crisco oil. Stir in one-half to one cup of fresh chopped dill.

Serve on top of light rye or whole wheat bread, sliced fairly thin, with the gravlax.

Or put out a platter of the sliced gravlax, a tray of bread and a bowl of the sauce, and let your guests serve themselves. Watch them hesitate, then wheel around for quick seconds.

EVERYONE'S HOT CRAB DIP

Combine all but the crab meat and almonds in a cuisinart and blend well.

Then place in a bowl and mix in the crab meat.

Place in an oven-proof dish. Sprinkle with sliced almonds. This mixture will bubble up in the oven – so do not fill the dish beyond 2/3 capacity.

Bake at 375 degrees F for 15 minutes.

Serve with Triscuits, or French bread, or any crackers you prefer. Best to cool for a few minutes before serving. It will freeze well cooked or uncooked.

This is everyone's favourite crab dip, and we include it in case you have not got your copy of this recipe.

8 ounces cream cheese

1 tablespoon cream

2 tablespoons onion, chopped fine

1/2 teaspoon horseradish sauce

1/4 teaspoon salt

8 ounces fresh crab meat

Sliced almonds

Gravlax

SASKATCHEWAN

The Prairies are stunning in their beauty, in all seasons. No one appreciated the Canadian Prairies more than Bruno.

Although raised under the shadow of the mountains in Exshaw, Alberta, until age seven, and then in view of the mountains in New Westminster, Bruno always reminded interviewers he was born in Medicine Hat, Alberta. He loved the Prairies and understood completely when I said my body would suffer a chemical imbalance if my feet were not on Prairie soil at least once every year.

The animal life of the Prairies fascinated Bruno. On our drives to Saskatchewan, there would be the beige and white-assed little antelope near Medicine Hat, and the side-of-the-road snoopy gophers on hind legs.

We counted hunched-over hawks on the telephone poles, saw scrawny coyotes and elegant deer, and once, a den of irresistible red fox cubs playing near the side of a farm road. We laughed over the kid-loving farm dog who hated pigs; and Bruno could not take enough pictures of the rare osprey nest on top of the grain elevator near Preeceville, and the menacing, circling-ever-lower parent birds who were not pleased as he got nearer the elevator and the nest. We spent a hilarious afternoon last summer driving over several back forties looking for Ken and Elsa Laxdal's herd of buffalo, who had cleverly hidden all 140 of themselves.

Bruno, Preeceville, Saskatchewan

That same afternoon, the big Prairie sky boiled up some dark and threatening clouds, framed against the fields of ripening wheat and rapeseed. You could feel Bruno wishing for his sketch pad. He was beginning to take more time to sketch and paint, and every aspect of the Prairie landscape drew him.

Bruno marvelled at field after yellow field of rapeseed in flower, and he leaped out with the camera when we found a cornflower-blue field of flax in bloom beside the golden rapeseed. He understood when I suddenly stopped the car and ran back to berate a man picking the rare wild tiger lilies growing in the ditch. Although he said later he was glad he did not have to come and rescue me. I knew I was always safe with Bruno nearby. He gave me courage.

Bruno had a fierce pride in Canada – all parts of it. As an actor, he had travelled to every corner of this nation. His radio magic and poetry and television programs reached even the most isolated hamlets. Bruno felt at home in every province and territory. Saskatchewan was special because it was there that he took the time to relax the most, to let all pressure slip away. He was quietly part of the community, and when he died, the "Canora Courier" and "Norquay North Star" newspapers each published a full page, loving tribute to Bruno, written by Gary Lewchuk, that said the community "didn't say goodbye to the actor, they said goodbye to a friend."

Prairie Harvest

As a province, Saskatchewan has been in survival mode for most of its life. No great riches have ever made it financially comfy, and most Prairie stock still know how to grow their own vegetables, or at least how to can and preserve the harvest.

Throughout the summer and fall, there are market gardens and farmers' markets everywhere, and the best vegetables on earth, which taste like vegetables. Bruno and I had our favourite markets, depending on the day and the nearby town. He knew exactly where to find the table with the best cinnamon rolls at the Yorkton Market, and that was always his first stop. Homemade crabapple or chokecherry jellies, Saskatoon pies, bunches of sweet peas for the table centre, hand-crafted quilts, cottage industries all.

After a trip to the Cross Market Garden in Yorkton, an institution, our favourite lunch was a plate of yellow beans with butter, salt and pepper, and homemade rolls.

The food in this chapter tends to be very basic, what a friend calls "down home food."

SASKATCHEWAN BAKED BEANS

2 lbs. navy beans

3 quarts water

3/4 lb. salt pork

1 medium onion

3-1/2 tablespoons dry mustard

1 cup brown sugar

1/4 cup ketchup

Wash 2 pounds of navy beans well, then put them to soak in 3 quarts of soft water overnight. The next morning boil them in the same water until done, 30 minutes or more. When done, layer the beans and salt pork, which has been cut in 1/2 inch strips, in a bean pot and bury a peeled onion in the beans.

Mix the dry mustard, brown sugar and ketchup in some of the bean broth and put the mixture over the beans. Fill the bean pot with the remaining bean broth to within 1/2 inch from the top. After it has come to a boil in a 275 degree F oven, bake with the lid on. If there is not enough bean broth, use boiling soft water to supplement, and add more liquid at half time. Cook for 7 to 8 hours. Remove the onion before serving.

PORK ROAST WITH GLAZE

Uncooked pork roast

1-1/2 cups brown sugar

2 or 3 tablespoons vinegar

2 teaspoons dry mustard

1/8 teaspoon ginger

Cover the surface of the uncooked pork roast with the mixture of brown sugar, vinegar, dry mustard and ginger.

During the roasting, spoon the pan drippings over the meat, basting often. Cook the roast at 325 degrees F, 40 minutes for each pound.

CHILI FOR SISSIES

That was us. We did not have Tex-Mex palates, and this mild chili, borrowed largely from my sister Moira, was a frequent dish in our early entertaining years. For those of you who like killer chili, get the red chili peppers out and keep pouring, along with the Tabasco sauce.

In a large heavy pot, place the contents of the cans of tomatoes, beans and soup, the soya sauce and ketchup.

In a large frying pan or wok, place half the butter and sauté the onions until they begin to get soft, add the green peppers and shortly after that, add the mushrooms. Sauté all until slightly tender, and pour into the large heavy pot.

In the same large pan or wok, place the remainder of the butter and the ground beef. Salt and pepper the first mixture to taste, and the same with the beef. Add a pinch or two of sugar to the beef while it is sautéing over fairly high heat.

When the meat is brown and broken into small pieces, add the meat mixture into the heavy pot and stir everything together well.

Simmer in the heavy pot for an hour or longer, uncovered; or covered lightly but not tightly.

Serve with rice or broad noodles. Keep a small dish of hot red peppers nearby for the complainers.

1-1/2 lbs. lean ground beef

1 large onion, sliced and chopped

1 large green pepper, sliced and chopped

3/4 lb. fresh (or canned) mushrooms, sliced

2 tins red kidney beans

1 large tin of tomatoes, sliced

3 tablespoons ketchup

Salt and pepper to taste

1-1/2 teaspoon ground chili powder

1 teaspoon red chili peppers

1 dash of soya sauce

1 can tomato soup

3 tablespoons butter

Pinch or two of sugar

What Are You Doing Here?

It was a Prime Ministerial double-take, when Jean Chrétien saw Bruno at a large rally of Liberal supporters on a farm north of Yorkton. I had tried to talk Bruno out of attending, not wanting him to feel obligated to accompany me on my Liberal politicking, an activity I picked up at the age of six.

Bruno had gone with me to Liberal banquets in Vancouver, where he was always warmly greeted by Jean and Aline Chrétien. But we were at the cottage in Saskatchewan this time, it was an hour's drive to the rally, and the day was ideal for golf. No, he was quietly insistent. He wanted to go. It was not until later that he told me he and the Prime Minster had known one another for many years, at least back to when Bruno was doing the radio show in the '60s, and Jean Chrétien was a young politician in Ottawa.

My ever-present camera was there for Bruno to take a picture of me with the Prime Minister, which now hangs on my wall, but the best shots of the day were of Bruno with the gracious Aline Chrétien, a quiet fan of his. Two of their grandchildren, Olivier and Maximillian Desmarais, were with the Chrétiens for that Saskatchewan trip.

Bruno and I both took our politics seriously, and while we supported different parties, we always liked the same people in politics, regardless of party affiliations, loved political discussions, and could never understand those who were apolitical.

We were both glad we had taken the break from the Jam Factory and golfing for this day. It's not every day you have to explain your presence to the Prime Minister in the middle of a wheat field.

Opposite photo: Aline Chrétien, Bruno, Olivier and Maximillian Desmarais

N A N C Y ' S H O M E M A D E S A U S A G E M E A T

1 lb. of coarsely ground pork

2/3 cup bread crumbs (large soft crumbs, not fine ones)

1/4 cup water

1-1/2 to 2 teaspoons of sage

1/8 teaspoon sugar

1/8 teaspoon ground coriander

1/8 teaspoon ground cardamom

1/4 teaspoon pepper

1/2 teaspoon salt

Place all the ingredients into a bowl and mix well. Form into meat patties and fry as you would any sausage.

Makes approximately 8 large patties.

This recipe can be made heart-smart by substituting ground turkey for the ground pork. The taste is the same, the texture very similar. And Bruno, the eternal sausage lover, liked the turkey substitute as much as he did the pork sausage.

Sour Cream

*Nancy – barefoot
in the kitchen*

Throughout the book, there are a number of recipes that call for cream-that-has-gone-sour.

The milkman delivered the milk, but you went to the farm to get the cream. You took a clean glass sealer jar to the farmer's wife, and she poured thick cream from the cans into it for you. She waited for the foam to settle down a bit so she could fill the sealer up to the top. Much like pouring a glass of champagne.

Then there it was, thick cream for desserts, baking, your coffee, but most of all, poured over fresh berries.

*There were always two sealers of cream in the refrigerator. One fresh that week, and the unused cream, which before too long had gone sour. You might throw out sour milk, but **never** sour cream. Far too many recipes just cry for it. And these were the recipes of our mothers and grandmothers, designed to make use of sour cream, before the days when all milk and cream became pasteurized.*

To duplicate these recipes today, you cannot use homogenized, store bought sour cream. It does not work. The natural chemicals are not the same.

*The days of the quart of cream from the farm exist only in rural areas. What do you do for sour cream in the city? You plan ahead. You buy whipping cream and let it go sour. (It is suspicious how long it takes commercial whipping cream to go sour. What **are** those additives?)*

So you have to be patient, plan ahead, and have the real cream go sour naturally. It is worth the wait.

VEAL CUTLETS IN SOUR CREAM

Our friend, Lauris Talmey, insists that if you are going to cook veal, it must be red veal and not white veal, because of the inhumane way that white veal is produced.

So begin with any cut of red veal, either cutlets, chops or shanks. Vary the cooking time according to the cut of the meat: the less expensive the cut, the longer and slower the cooking time in order to tenderize it.

Braise the veal on both sides in a small amount of butter and olive oil in a frying pan. Then place in an oven-proof heavy casserole dish. Salt and pepper.

Add the sour cream to the frying pan; let it bubble, and scrape out the contents of the pan, pour over the veal, and cook covered for about an hour in 300 degree F oven. Then uncovered for 15 minutes at 350.

Bruno was known to snitch this while it was still warm, or cold, into a sandwich.

1 lb. veal, thickly cut

1 tablespoon butter

1 tablespoon olive oil

Salt and pepper to taste

2/3 cup cream-that-has-gone-sour

Nancy and Bruno

VEGETABLES ONLY

A Streetcar Named Desire

Bruno at one of Dr. Foth's infamous birthday parties on Bowen Island

Bruno and The West Coast

While the vitality, diversity and excitement of Toronto fueled Bruno's energy, and more important, his children and grandchildren were in Toronto, it is the West that ultimately claimed him.

*Raised in Exshaw, Alberta, and New Westminster, British Columbia, Bruno's early years of theatre and radio drama were in the West. A scholarship to the Banff School of Fine Arts was followed by three years in the Seattle Repertory Theatre. On his return to Vancouver, audiences still recall Bruno's riveting performances at the Everyman and Totem Theatres and Theatre Under the Stars - George in Steinbeck's **Of Mice and Men,** Tom in **The Glass Menagerie** and Stanley Kowalski in **A Streetcar Named Desire**, pictured here with Murial Ontkean.*

Tyrone Guthrie lured Bruno east to join the talent at Stratford, where, for 12 years, Bruno gave one memorable performance after another - including a brilliant Feste in **Twelfth Night**, Marc Antony in **Julius Caesar**, the lead in **Peer Gynt** and the hot-blooded, sensual portrayal of Romeo in **Romeo and Juliet**. In a tribute to Bruno on the Internet, Dan MacDonald recalled Bruno's Romeo: "... The performance still lives, in almost mythic proportions, in the memories of all those who saw it."

Ida, Bruno's young wife, died tragically while they were at Stratford, and Bruno became a single Dad for Rico, age 11, and Tina, 8. He moved to Toronto to provide a stable home to raise his children, where for four years he hosted "Gerussi!", the nationwide, three hour morning radio show that changed radio in Canada.

But the West was waiting to reclaim a native son. In 1971, "Beachcombers" began filming at Gibsons, B.C., and the glorious west coast setting was soon to be seen in over 50 countries, as Bruno starred in the longest-running, most successful series in CBC television history. It ran for 19 years before the suits in Toronto pulled the plug – a corporate decision right up there with the introduction of the doomed and ill-advised "new" Coca-Cola.

Bruno and Jackson Davies -
last month of filming **"The Beachcombers"**

Bruno and Tony Pantages
Yellowpoint, B.C.

EASY CORN CHOWDER

We have taken these ingredients out on a boat trip, or on a golf holiday. The ingredients travel well because they are not perishable, and it only take a few minutes to assemble and cook.

1 can creamed corn

1/2 can lima beans, drained

1/2 onion, chopped

1 can condensed milk

Salt and pepper to taste

5 or 6 cloves

Drain the lima beans. Sauté the chopped onion in butter. Add a small amount of water and simmer to soften and cook the onions.

Combine all of the ingredients, and heat gently.

Do not let boil.

Bruno finally had time for some serious golf. He loved the beauty and the richness of life in British Columbia, and although he still owned a house in Toronto, as well as in Gibsons, it was the West Coast that was home, and where his heart remained.

Bruno, David Sims, Hugh Lyons

Golfing between wine-tasting sessions in the Napa Valley May, 1994.

Nancy, Jacquie and Sandra in the Napa Valley burning up the golf course

TENDER DANDELION GREENS

Bruno's Mother, Nona, knew what many of our parents and grandparents knew - that fresh dandelion greens were a treat, especially with the young green leaves in the spring, and a therapeutic treat as well.

As an herb, the dandelion has been used traditionally in herbal teas, to aid digestion and as a mild laxative, or in herbal baths or skin tonics.

Bruno's memories of Nona's dandelion greens were many and fond.

As with any greens, you can add further ingredients according to your preference - cooked bacon bits, croutons, garlic or plain, chopped boiled egg, parmesan cheese or green onions.

2 cups fresh dandelion leaves

Salt and ground pepper to taste

3 tablespoons olive oil

1 tablespoon vinegar

Wash and spin or towel dry the dandelion leaves. Break into bite size pieces.

Place leaves in a salad bowl, season with salt and pepper.

Add oil and vinegar and mix gently to coat the greens.

PICKLED BEETS

Bruno understood my Mother's devotion to pickles and beets. These were a constant on Jessie's table.

15 to 16 medium sized beets, approximately 3-1/2 pounds

2 cups white vinegar

2 cups brown sugar

1 cup water

Boil the beets until cooked (a fork goes through fairly easily), drain, cool with cold water, then skin them.

Pack the beets in sterilized sealers.

Boil together the vinegar, brown sugar and one cup of water. Pour this mixture hot over the beets so it permeates them. Seal the jars.

Sandy and Hugh Lyons,
Nancy and Bruno.
Palm Springs 1991.

BRUNO'S WHISTLER CARROTS

*Bruno – reaching for the sharpening
steel at his 65th birthday bash in
West Vancouver, May 7, 1993.*

After a day of the legendary Man of the Mountains, Jim McConkey, skiing Bruno's tush all over Whistler Mountain, we were doing après ski and dinner at McConkey's. The fireplace was on, the steaks were ready to barbecue, and Bruno volunteered to do the vegetables.

---

1 large onion

8 large carrots, peeled, cut in
    2 inch lengths

2 large red sweet peppers, cored
    and seeds removed

1 to 2 tablespoons butter or
    olive oil

With a sharp knife and great precision, Bruno cut all 3 vegetables in approximately 2 inch long, finely thin, julienne slices. He put everything together into a large frying pan with the butter – and just kept turning them, over a medium-high heat.

The vegetables were done in minutes. It was visually a wonderful combination, with taste to match.

COOKED SALAD DRESSING

"We had one rule – we had to have fun. We would eat, we would drink, we would gesture... we'd call it our 'talian aerobics." Jackson Davies

Beat the eggs well, add the sugar, salt, mustard, flour and continue until thoroughly blended.

Heat vinegar to boiling, pour over the egg mixture and continue beating all the time.

Add sour cream and butter and cook in double boiler until dressing is thick and smooth, stirring all the time.

2 eggs
4 tablespoons sugar
1 teaspoon salt
1 tablespoon butter
1-1/2 cups cream-that-has-
   gone-sour
3 tablespoons flour
1 teaspoon mustard
1/4 cup vinegar

Photo:

Prairie flowers; Jacquie, Bruno and Nancy in the rapeseed. The next day the farmer posted a "no trespassing" sign.

*Maureen Keith and
Bruno at one of her
famous Taurus parties.*

CHILLED
TOMATO
SOUP

You should only do this once a year – because it is sinful. Save it for the hottest, muggiest day when cooking is out of the question.

I always associate this recipe with Bruno, because it was served many years ago at a lunch given by Mary Sims in Kitchener, to a group of us en route to Stratford. David Sims, Mary's son, is married to Jacquie Vaughan Sims, my unofficial sister and dear friend. They were courting then. I was in awe of a young actor at Stratford whose presence dominated the stage, and whom I would not meet until years later.

1 can tomato soup

1/2 soup can milk

1/2 soup can heavy cream

1/4 cup fresh chopped chives

In a bowl, place the soup, and fill the empty can 1/2 with milk and top up with heavy cream. Beat all together well. Refrigerate for a couple of hours, beat again before serving. Top with chopped chives. This is deceptively simple. the whipping and chilling give the soup a texture all its own.

Serves 4.

CHEESE LOVERS' POTATOES

3/4 cup grated cheddar cheese
1 pint milk
2 tablespoons butter
2 tablespoons flour
4 cups of potatoes
Pinch of nutmeg
Pinch of salt
Pinch of sugar

Skin and cube the potatoes, which have been boiled in their skins and cooled. Put the potatoes in a baking dish that has been buttered.

Make a cheese sauce by melting the butter over medium heat, then adding the flour, salt, nutmeg and sugar; when that mixture bubbles, add the milk and grated cheese. Stir over medium heat until smooth and fairly thick.

Parmesan cheese can also be added for a sharper taste.

Cover the potatoes with the cheese sauce and place some buttered bread crumbs on top.

Bake in 350 degree F oven until the sauce and the potatoes are piping hot.

Great served with baked ham.

CANDIED SWEET POTATOES

4 medium sized sweet potatoes, baked
  and peeled
1/2 cup white sugar
1/2 cup water
1/2 cup brown sugar
1/2 cup butter

Bake or boil the sweet potatoes until they are almost done, then peel and cut into serving size pieces. Place in buttered casserole and cover with the syrup made as follows:

Combine the sugar, water, brown sugar and butter together, and pour over the sweet potatoes.

Bake in a 300 to 350 degree F oven for 1-1/2 hours, basting or turning the potatoes in the syrup at intervals.

MADELEINE'S STUFFED MUSHROOMS

Bruno and Bruce Gorman

20 large mushrooms

1/4 cup butter

1-1/2 tablespoon onion, chopped fine

2 eggs

1/2 cup breadcrumbs

Pinch of nutmeg

Salt and pepper to taste

3 or 4 grated tablespoons grated Parmesan cheese

Wash the mushrooms, cut out and chop stems and set aside.

Melt the butter in a pan, and sauté the chopped mushroom stems and chopped onion.

Beat the eggs and mix with the breadcrumbs.

Add the sautéed mushroom and onion mixture.

Add salt, pepper and a touch of nutmeg.

Fill the mushroom crowns with the mixture and top with Parmesan cheese.

Bake 20 minutes at 375 degrees F in a buttered dish or baking sheet.

Madeleine Shaw made these for a party at the Shaw home years ago. She generously shared the recipe, and we have enjoyed it over the years.

CHICKEN AND EGGS

CHICKEN OR TURKEY STUFFING

My Dad used to tease my Mom. "If the chickens ever go on strike, your mother is in serious trouble."

This is a big batch of stuffing. If you have a large wok – use it. Otherwise, do the sautéing in your biggest frying pan, and then mix the ingredients from the frying pan with bread crumbs in your biggest mixing bowl.

In the large pan or wok melt the butter and sauté the onions until almost soft. Add the celery and apples and sauté for a couple of minutes. Then add all the seasonings, and mix well.

Place seven to eight cups of bread crumbs in the large mixing bowl, or directly into the wok, if that is what you are using. Mix well with the ingredients that you have just sautéed.

Use what you need for the bird at hand, and freeze the remainder in individual one cup packages for later use.

1/2 cup butter
1 large sweet onion, chopped fine
1 cup celery, chopped fine
(leaves, stalks, heart, whatever
you have)
2 apples, peeled, cored and
chopped fine
1/2 tablespoon ground sage
3 tablespoons parsley flakes
1-1/2 teaspoons poultry
seasoning
1 teaspoon salt
1 teaspoon ground pepper
Pinch of sugar
7 to 8 cups medium soft bread
crumbs (not the fine commercial
bread crumbs)

ROAST CHICKEN

First you have to overcome that yucky feeling of putting your hand inside the bird and making sure that the packages of giblets are out of the cavity, and anything else that should be pulled loose is discarded. (Bruno was fearless, but sometimes forgetful.) Then wash the bird thoroughly under cold water, inside and out, and dry with paper towelling. Rub the inside of the cavity with half a lemon, then sprinkle the cavity with a bit of salt. Place your dressing inside, and either secure the flaps to the cavity with small skewers, or double some tinfoil and place it over the opening to the cavity to prevent the stuffing from coming out during the roasting. June O'Connor blocks the opening with an apple.

If there was excess fat at the entrance to the cavity, make sure you save it and place it either on top of the bird or in the pan to provide extra fat for basting. Or you can place a tablespoon or two of butter or olive oil on the bird.

Roast chicken is comfort food, and it seems to work best on a rainy or stormy afternoon. Put in a slow oven so the smell can permeate the house. The smell also reminds you to go and baste the chicken well, every time you pass through the kitchen.

You can roast the chicken all afternoon in a 300 degree F oven for 3 or 4 hours, if it is a fairly large bird. Or use a hotter oven for a shorter time if your timetable dictates. The bird is done when you wiggle one of the legs and it feels loose. Some prefer their chicken done less, but that is our test if you like fowl that comes fairly easily off the bone.

Serve with small, new potatoes, and your favourite vegetables. For an added touch, Bruno prized crabapple jelly, made and sold by the farmers at the local markets in Saskatchewan. There are also commercial brands of crabapple jelly.

ROAST TURKEY

Use the same procedure and stuffing for a turkey as for roast chicken, with the addition of stuffing the crop (the end opposite the open cavity, the end from which the neck has been removed) with homemade sausage. Pack the sausage, uncooked, tight into that cavity, and secure the loose flap of skin over the sausage meat with metal skewers. You can use either pork or turkey sausage. When serving the turkey, simply slice pieces of the sausage meat to serve along with the turkey meat.

And remember, if you are cooking a turkey, plan to stick around for most of the day. Stuff the bird in the morning, and put it in the oven early enough to allow sufficient hours of cooking, if you are going to do it the slow, uncovered way – and keep basting.

*Sycamouse loved
chicken and Bruno*

"Waste not, want not," mottoed my Mother.

Bruno's fondness for roast chicken extended to the chicken soup that always resulted from the carcass and drippings. Nothing goes to waste when you roast a chicken. And Bruno was an enthusiast for the time-saving stuffing we usually made in one big batch and froze in smaller, one cup packages – ready to pop into the cavity before roasting. Small bird, one package; Big turkey, several packages.

Or, if time was short, and there was no stuffing left in the freezer, Bruno would just rub the chicken cavity with half a lemon, and stuff the chicken with slices of onion, celery and apple, and sprinkle generous shakes of parsley, sage, poultry seasoning, salt and pepper into the cavity before roasting. You can add or substitute your favourite seasonings - rosemary, thyme, tarragon, or savory, for example.

Thanks to the Cuisinart and stale bread from time to time, there was always a supply of bread crumbs stored in the freezer.

CHICKEN SOUP

After a meal of roast chicken, placing the remainder of the chicken carcass in the fridge always seemed cumbersome, and possibly dangerous, because of the warnings our mothers gave us about never keeping chicken or turkey stuffing in the carcass after the bird is cooked. So we have always stripped the carcass of the remaining meat, placing the meat in foil or a plastic bag – easy to store in the fridge – and placed the balance of the stuffing in a separate container. There you have makings of your chicken sandwiches for the next picnic.

Don't be shy about leaving some stuffing clinging to the cavity. Place the stripped carcass into your big soup pot, including the skin and bones that you have stripped of meat. And most important, all the drippings from the original roasting pan, saved and scraped into the soup pot. Cover the carcass and bones with water; add a chopped onion, a few chopped carrots, a chopped potato, cleaned with skin still on, salt and pepper, a couple of tablespoons of parsley, one or two bay leaves; cover and simmer for a few hours. If you have a really low element on your stove, you can simmer, covered, overnight.

Let cool, strain and skim off the fat. You can salvage the potato without the skin, the carrots and the onion for processing to help thicken the soup later, but at this stage, you have a fairly rich chicken stock.

Then I cheat. I whisk into the stock, which has been put back into the big soup pot, one or two packages of dry soup mix. Our preferences were either one onion and one cream of chicken, or the chicken and red bell pepper, Knorr preferred. Or use the stock to make one of your favourite soups.

If you are using the soup mixes, make sure you follow the directions on the package, and whisk the dry ingredients well into the soup stock. Let it boil for a couple of minutes and then simmer for five minutes or longer.

CHICKEN TARRAGON

1 chicken, cut into pieces for frying

1 tablespoon butter

2 tablespoons olive oil

1 to 1-1/2 tablespoons tarragon

Salt and pepper to taste

1/2 cup heavy cream-that-has-gone-sour

Sauté the chicken in the butter and olive oil. While it sautées over a fairly high heat, sprinkle salt and pepper and a generous amount of tarragon all over both sides of the chicken as you turn it.

When sautéed brown, remove and place in casserole dish. Add the sour cream to the frying pan, let it cook for a minute, scraping the juices and brown bits from the pan. Then pour the contents of the frying pan over the chicken. Place in a 325 degree F oven, covered for 1/2 hour and uncovered for 1/2 hour.

This dish can be cooked in a slower oven for a longer period of time, or a hotter oven for a shorter period of time, depending on your own timetable. It is best cooked slowly.

The Kitchen Gods

It's nice not to have screw-ups in the kitchen – but we all have them. When the great restaurateur and chef, Umberto Menghi, is coming for dinner, the pressure is on. When he brings his family, who are visiting from Italy, including Mamma Delia, the inspiration of Umberto's culinary wizardry – you hope your kitchen gods are not away on a frolic.

This particular night, the gods stuck around for Bruno, but left me on my own.

Our first course was Bruno cooking Umberto's prawns. They were done to perfection. Umberto raved, "Bruno, how did you do these? They are wonderful." Great laughter when Bruno told him, "It's your recipe." And the gracious Umberto said, "Well, you do it better than me."

The main course was chicken tarragon, which I had prepared. Now I like fowl to fall fairly easily from the bone, but this dish had been left in the oven so long, the bones themselves were falling apart, to my horror. Fickle kitchen gods out doing the town.

Salvation came with Norwegian cream for dessert and "Bravissimo" from Umberto, who well knew the dinner needed saving.

CHEESE SOUFFLÉ WITH LOVE

A FAVOURITE SUPPER

Bruno was a light eater, and he was a sucker for anything with cheese in it. When fresh asparagus arrived in the spring, one of our frequent and very favourite suppers was a cheese soufflé, with James Beard's quick hollandaise sauce, and fresh asparagus. Followed by either fresh strawberries or a pear.

We both loved soufflés, and tried not to be intimidated by them. Like a dog, if the soufflé knew you were afraid it could turn into a bully. Bruno never did scare easily.

Pre-heat oven to 375 degrees F.

Prepare a soufflé dish with a light coating of butter, then dust with flour.

Make a white sauce by melting the butter, adding the flour, let it bubble for a few minutes. Add the nutmeg, salt, pepper and mustard and stir. Stir the milk in gradually

Separate the eggs and put two egg yolks to one side. Put the remaining egg yolks one at a time into the white sauce mixture, stirring continuously. Then stir in the cheese.

Add the cream of tartar to the egg whites, and beat egg whites until stiff. Then fold the egg whites into the cheese mixture, and place in the prepared soufflé dish.

Bake for 20 to 25 minutes, until the soufflé has risen and is crusty golden on the top. Serve immediately with hollandaise sauce.

3 tablespoons butter

3-1/2 tablespoons flour

1-1/4 cups milk

6 eggs

Pinch of salt

Pinch of sugar

1/8 teaspoon cream of tartar

1/3 grated Swiss cheese

1/3 cup Parmesan cheese

1/3 cup cheddar cheese

1 teaspoon dry mustard

Pinch of nutmeg

Pepper to taste or pinch of
Cayenne pepper

JAMES BEARD'S
QUICK HOLLANDAISE SAUCE

James Beard took the mystery out of hollandaise sauce for me for over 30 years ago with this recipe from

The James Beard Cookbook, *published by Dell Publishing Co. Inc. in 1959. My first edition paperback,*

purchased that year for 75 cents, remains one of the treasured, if tattered, volumes on my bookshelves.

---

3 egg yolks

2 teaspoons fresh lemon juice

1 teaspoon salt

Pinch of Cayenne pepper

1/3 to 1/2 cup melted butter

Place the egg yolks in a blender with the lemon juice, 1/2 teaspoon salt and a few grains of Cayenne pepper. Blend quickly. Then add hot melted butter to the mixture while the blender is on high speed.

The mixture will blend and thicken. Serve immediately.

BRUNO'S CLEAN-OUT-THE-FRIDGE OMELETTE

Bruno was an intuitive cook, never bound by the mere perimeters of a recipe. The courage, artistry and passion that he displayed in his life and his art were also present in his cooking. One of the first meals he ever cooked for me was an omelette, where he simply opened the fridge door, said, "What's in here?" and began.

First he put a dab of butter in a small frying pan, and cut up two small tomatoes. Bruno preferred Roma tomatoes. He sprinkled a pinch of sugar, some salt and pepper and basil on top of the tomatoes, brought them to a quick boil, reduced the heat to simmer and poured onto the tomatoes a generous tablespoon or two of brandy.

(Hey! Is the sun over the yardarm?)

Next he choppped some onion, green and red peppers, and mushrooms. Into another skillet he placed another dab of butter and the onions and the peppers, sautéeing them over medium to high heat until they began to cook. Then he added mushrooms, stirring them all together. He sprinkled that mixture with a touch more basil and some oregano.

He shredded 3 or 4 tablespoons of cheddar cheese and added some Parmesan cheese, and set that aside. There was some left over ham in the fridge, which he diced, and put into the onion, pepper and mushroom mixture.

He whisked 4 eggs together with a teaspoon of water for each two eggs, added salt and pepper to taste, and a pinch of nutmeg. He put the eggs in the omelette pan which was medium hot and had a coating of butter. As the egg mixture began to bubble, Bruno lifted the edges to allow the mixture to run underneath and cook, so that the top of the omelette always remained soft. At just the right stage, when the eggs were almost cooked through, he placed along the top of one-half of the omelette the tomato mixture, the onion, pepper, mushroom and ham mixture, the shredded cheddar and Parmesan cheese. Then the other half was folded over and a most glorious omelette was served.

That omelette varied over the years: whatever happened to be in the fridge. It could have been bacon or homemade sausage instead of ham. If there were cooked potatoes, some slices were bound to end up in the omelette. There was never any set ingredient or measurement.

After that first omelette, I knew I was in the presence of a cook.

4 eggs

3 tablespoons butter

2 small tomatoes, chopped

3 tablespoons cheddar cheese, grated

1 tablespoon Parmesan cheese, grated

Chopped ham, bacon or sausage

2 or 3 tablespoons onion, chopped

2 or 3 tablespoons red and green peppers, chopped

2 tablespoons mushrooms, chopped

Pinch of sugar

Salt and pepper to taste

2 tablespoons brandy

Basil to taste

Oregano to taste

Pinch of nutmeg

SWEET PEPPER FRITTATA FOR TWO

Pre-heat oven to broil.

3 eggs
2 teaspoons water
2 tablespoons butter
2 or 3 tablespoons sweet* onion,
    chopped fine
2 to 3 tablespoons sweet pepper, chopped fine
    (red, orange, or yellow pepper)
2 tablespoons grated Parmesan cheese

Two frying pans make this quicker to prepare.

In one pan put 1 tablespoon of butter and sauté the onion until it begins to get a bit soft, then add the chopped sweet pepper. Sauté both until almost cooked.

While the onions and peppers cook over medium heat, melt the remaining tablespoon of butter in a small frying pan or a small omelette pan over medium heat. Beat the eggs with the water and pour into the omelette pan. Lift the edges of the eggs as they begin to cook, to allow the liquid eggs to run underneath, as if you were cooking an omelette. When the top of the eggs is still moist, but close to being cooked, spread the grated Parmesan cheese over the top of the eggs, then spread the onions and peppers over the top of that.

Put the pan on the top rack of the oven, just under the broiler, for a minute or two, and serve.

You can season the eggs with salt and pepper prior to cooking them, or season to taste after the frittata is cooked.

*The large Spanish onion, or Maui, Walla Walla, or Vidalia onion, if available.

COUNTRY FRITTATA

This is really the open-faced version of Bruno's "Clean-Out-the-Fridge-Omelette."

Instead of completing this dish as an omelette, simply pre-heat the oven to broil and prepare whatever toppings you want. The tomatoes stewed in brandy and basil as described in Bruno's omelette are always a welcome addition to a frittata. Cheese of almost any description is a must. But basically, use whatever topping you feel like, or have on hand.

Allow about two eggs per person, and once you have prepared the toppings and spread them over the top of the frittata, run the frittata under the broiler for a few minutes to finish cooking the eggs, which should still be moist before you broil.

We have been known to sauté the onion and peppers the night before, particularly if we had guests and an early tee time at the golf course.

Our Last Game

Our last golf game together was September 3, 1995, during the Labour Day weekend, the day we were to attend Dr. Foth's famous annual birthday party. It was an early morning game at Furry Creek Golf and Country Club, north of Vancouver, where bears have been known to critique your golf swing, and long trails up spectacular mountain cart paths distract the most serious golfer.

To the amazement of both Bruno and myself, I birdied the first hole and made my first hole-in-one on the second hole. "Remind me to buy a lottery ticket today," said I, still stunned at such a start. "This must be my lucky day." Then I fell on the steep, dew-laden slope coming off the fourth green and broke my right leg, badly.

En route to the hospital, I told the ambulance guys to step on it. We had a party to attend. The ambulance attendants just smiled, while Bruno looked a bit frantic. We never did see Fotheringham. They let me out of the hospital one week later, leg pinned and paining, with pneumonia as a bonus.

Bruno became the sole cook, nurse, shopper, chauffeur, housekeeper and entertainer for the next six weeks. His food trays, to tempt the petulant, were works of art. His patience and humour were sublime, although he did do some wicked imitations of my petty demands. He called himself Florence, or "Flo" for short. He was wonderful.

During those days, he produced my favourite comfort foods, including scrambled eggs, and we began to work seriously on this cookbook. Looking back, the word serendipitous comes to mind.

BEGINNER'S
SCRAMBLED EGGS

When you are making scrambled eggs, slow down. Use the lowest heat you can, and do not rush the cooking.

Beat the eggs together with the water and seasonings. (Water makes for softer eggs than milk).

Place a small amount of butter in your frying pan over low heat. And keep the heat low throughout. Pour the eggs into the pan, and give them a gentle stir from time to time. If you keep the cooking slow, your eggs will be soft, without the trace of water that results when you have cooked the eggs too quickly over high heat.

Bruno's deft touch with eggs equalled his skill with seafood.

2 eggs per person

1 or 2 teaspoons of water for every 2 eggs

Salt and pepper to taste

Pinch of nutmeg

BREAKFAST BREADS
AND MUFFINS

The Gerussi eyebrows were the most expressive in show business. They always got a workout when I murmured we should open a bed and breakfast. His idea of hell would be eating breakfast daily with strangers. But he was very partial to breakfast breads and muffins. Here are some of his favourites.

PATTEE'S BANANA MUFFINS

Preheat oven to 375 degrees F.

3 large bananas

3/4 cup sugar

1 egg

1 teaspoon baking soda

1 teaspoon baking powder

1/2 teaspoon salt

1-1/2 cups flour

1/3 cup melted butter

Mash the bananas. Add the sugar and the slightly beaten egg.

Add the melted butter. Stir in the dry ingredients.

Place in individual papered muffin tins. Bake for 20 minutes in 375 degrees F oven.

One of our best ever neighbours at Crystal Lake, Pattee Flett, turned us on to these muffins.

ORANGE MUFFINS

Preheat oven to 350 degrees F and grease muffin tins.

1/4 cup butter

1/2 cup sugar

1 egg

Juice and rind of one orange

2 cups flour

1 teaspoon baking soda

1 teaspoon baking powder

1/2 cup milk-that-has-gone-sour

1 cup cut-up dates (optional)

Blend well the butter, sugar and egg. Then add the orange rind and juice. Sift the flour, soda and baking powder together. Fold the flour and sour milk alternately into the first mixture. Mix by hand, not machine, and do not overmix. Add dates.

Bake at 350 degrees F for 20 to 25 minutes in individual muffin tins. Makes 12 large muffins.

While still hot from the oven, brush over the top a mixture of additional orange juice and melted sugar made from:

2 tablespoons icing sugar

1 tablespoon orange juice

BANANA NUT LOAF

Preheat oven to 350 degrees F and grease 2 muffin tins.

1/2 cup butter, soft
2 cups white sugar
2 eggs
1/2 teaspoon salt
6 bananas, mashed
3 cups flour
2 teaspoons baking soda
1/2 teaspoon baking powder
2/3 cup chopped pecans

Cream together the sugar, butter, eggs and salt, beating well.

Stir in the mashed bananas.

Sift together the flour, baking soda and baking powder. Stir these dry ingredients into the above mixture. Add the pecans.

Put into two buttered loaf pans. Bake for 1 hour at 350 degrees F. Let stand for 1/2 hour before turning out of the pans.

This is a double recipe – so there is one loaf to slip into the freezer. Bruno never let these loaves linger long. A favourite breakfast snack, and his sugar hit on the golf course.

THERESA'S BREAD

This is for bread machines only.

1 cup whole wheat flour
1 cup white flour
1 teaspoon white sugar
2 tablespoons demerara sugar
1 tablespoon sunflower seeds
1 tablespoon flax seeds
1 tablespoon butter
1 teaspoon salt
3/4 cup water
1-1/4 teaspoons yeast (preferably Oetker)

Place yeast in pan first, then the flour and other ingredients. Make sure the yeast and salt are not together.

Bake at the whole wheat setting, usually 5 hours.

Bruno and I finally succumbed to a bread machine after many gifts of warm bread from Theresa and Ed Odishaw. This is basically Theresa's recipe, with some slight variations to indulge Bruno's fondness for demerara sugar.

And we adopted Theresa's time-saving method of keeping the dry ingredients pre-mixed in individual packages in the freezer.

GRAHAM GEMS

Preheat oven to 375 degrees F

1/2 cup butter

1 cup light brown sugar

2 eggs

2 cups cream-that-has-gone-sour

1/2 cup flour

Pinch of salt

1/4 teaspoon baking powder

1 teaspoon baking soda

1-2/3 cups graham flour

Combine the butter, sugar and eggs and beat well. Sift together the 1/2 cup of flour, the baking powder, soda and salt.

Add these dry ingredients to the graham flour. Now add the sour cream and all dry ingredients to the first mixture alternately. Do not overmix.

Spoon into greased muffin tins or paper muffin cups, about 2/3 filled.

Bake at 375 degrees for 15 to 20 minutes, until golden brown.

SUMMER FRUIT BUTTER

1 cup butter, softened

3/4 cup white sugar

The rind and juice of 1 lemon and 1 orange

Zest the rind of the lemon and orange. Combine all the ingredients and place in a glass jar and keep refrigerated.

Terrific on graham gems.

Nancy and Bruno at a Four Seasons
dinner party. Some devil put all
those glasses in front of us!

D U N F O R D ' S
F A V O U R I T E
C O F F E E   C A K E

It was Gary Dunford who was caught slipping his magic poetry under the door of Bruno's radio studio in the late '60s, when "Gerussi" ruled the airwaves.

Grease an angel food tin with butter. Pre-heat oven to 350 degrees F.

1/2 cup soft butter

1 cup white sugar

2 eggs

1/2 cup cream-that-has-gone-sour

1 tablespoon milk

1 teaspoon vanilla

1 teaspoon baking soda

2 teaspoons baking powder

1-2/3 cup flour

Topping

1/2 cup brown sugar
2 teaspoons cinnamon
1/2 cup chopped pecans

Cream together the butter, sugar and eggs, beating well. Add the sour cream and milk.

Sift together the flour, baking powder and baking soda. Stir into the above mixture, then add vanilla.

Pour half this cake batter into the greased angel food or bundt tin. Mix the three ingredients of the topping together, and sprinkle half of the topping over half of the cake batter.

Add the remaining cake batter, then put the remainder of the topping mixture on top.

Bake for 45 minutes in a 350 degree F oven.
Let cool before removing from the pan.

THE JAM FACTORY

"The Jam Factory" is the cottage at Crystal Lake, Saskatchewan, where what began as a small batch of fresh berry jam grew to a production line in later years.

My fascination with jam began with Jessie, my mother. When my sister, Moira, and I were little, we came upon a small patch of wild strawberries at the Lake. Mom persuaded us to forego the instant pleasure of eating them all immediately – and she made jam from one overflowing cup of those incredibly sweet, small berries.

The jam took only a few minutes to make, and I will never forget the taste or the colour, or the reality that those few berries made a jar of jam that lasted for several breakfasts.

Bruno was intrigued with the ease of jam-making, and became an expert. One summer we had his two oldest grandchildren at the Lake, Kenny and Syreeta Neal, and they too became jam enthusiasts. The enthusiasm has spread to the younger grandchildren, Liam, Graeme, Michaela and Esa, with the latest arrival in March 1996, Ellis Bruno Gerussi Turner still too young for such treats.

Because we were on vacation at the Lake, it was possible to get the fresh strawberries and small, almost wild raspberries from the farmers as soon as they were picked, and make the jam immediately.

The wild blueberries come in large, sealed wood flats, from the more northern parts of Saskatchewan and Manitoba; they are trucked to the great Secundiak's General Store in Stenen, Saskatchewan, where we and our golfing and Lake buddies tried to trick one another out of the earliest shipments.

*The Jam Factory –
the cottage at
Crystal Lake, Saskatchewan*

S T R A W B E R R Y   J A M

SASKATOON AND STRAWBERRY JAM

Two years ago we harvested pails of Saskatoon berries from the house at Gibsons, then tried making jam, using the recipe of four cups of fruit to four cups of sugar, preparing it in the same way as strawberry jam. The jam that resulted was very thick with an almost bitter taste.

So we tried mixing half and half with strawberry jam that had already been made which was quite runny. The strawberries did not have the amount of pectin that the Saskatoon berries did.

The result of mixing the two jams together was splendid, in both texture and taste.

The only trick is to be around when the temperamental Saskatoon berries are ready to be picked.

---

4 cups washed and cut up fresh
   strawberries

3-3/4 cups sugar

1 teaspoon butter

Pinch of salt

1 package Certo crystals

Place the strawberries in a heavy preserving pot over medium to high heat. Crush the berries with a potato masher, and as soon as the berries begin to bubble with the heat, add the sugar and salt and stir quickly with a wooden spoon to prevent any burning on the bottom of the pot.

(Make sure you are using a pot that has not been burned previously, or your jams will burn.)

Add 1 teaspoon of butter. This prevents foaming.

Bring to a quick boil, and as soon as the jam just begins to boil, add Certo crystals. Stir in immediately, and quickly bring the mixture to a full boil. When it has reached a boil that you cannot stir down, allow it to boil that rapidly for 1 minute and remove from the heat.

Wait until it cools and place in hot sterilized jars and seal.

Keep refrigerated.

RASPBERRY JAM

Use the same procedure as for strawberry jam. If the raspberries are not that sweet, add an extra 1/4 cup of sugar.

We never had to wonder what to give Gary Lauk for Christmas, once the raspberry jam was made.

PEACH JAM

Use the same procedure as for strawberry jam. If the peaches are really ripe and sweet, cut back a little on the sugar. If you boil too long, the jam becomes darker in color.

WILD BLUEBERRY JAM

4 cups wild blueberries, washed
4 cups sugar
1 teaspoon butter
Pinch of salt
1 package Certo crystals
2 tablespoons fresh squeezed lemon juice

First you have to find and clean those tiny, sweet and wonderful wild blueberries. You can substitute regular blueberries, but the taste is less exquisite.

Use the same procedure as you would for strawberry jam, with the exception of adding a couple of tablespoons of fresh squeezed lemon juice prior to the mixture's coming to a full boil.

This jam, as well as the strawberry jam and raspberry jam, is bright in colour and runny. Best stored in the refrigerator.

These jams also have another use. Heat a few tablespoons of your favourite flavour in the microwave, and pour over a scoop of ice cream.

Sandy and Jacquie at the Jam Factory, about to get their pay docked.

56

THE ANGE'S MARMALADE

Just so you are forewarned, this is a 48-hour recipe.

2 oranges

2 lemons

1 grapefruit

10 to 12 cups sugar

This recipe requires citrus fruits that are thin-skinned. They look shiny and smooth, not pebbled or puckered.

Wash the fruit and cut it into quarters, removing all seeds and the inner core, and pulverize in your food processor, skin and all.

Measure the fruit. To each cup of shredded fruit, add 3 cups of water. Let this mixture stand for 24 hours.

After the first 24 hours, boil the mixture hard for 10 minutes. Let it stand for another 24 hours.

Then to each cup of liquid, add 1 cup of sugar plus one additional cup for the pot.

Boil until it jells, approximately 15 to 20 minutes. To test for jelling, drip a small amount of the hot liquid on a saucer, place the saucer in the fridge for a minute or two and check to see how firm the marmalade is.

Place in hot sterilized jars and seal. This will make about 14 eight-ounce jars.

CRANBERRY ORANGE RELISH

1 lb. cranberries

2 cups sugar

1/2 cup water

Grated rind of 2 small oranges

Juice of 3 small oranges

1/2 cup blanched almonds, slivered

1 teaspoon butter

Place all but the almonds in a pot and cook until the cranberries pop open. It takes approximately 10 minutes.

To avoid foam during the cooking, add the butter. If foam persists, skim the foam from the surface.

Add the almonds and cool.

THE ANGE'S COOKBOOK

Bruno and I both marveled at the courage our parents and grandparents had in coming from their homes in distant countries to settle on the Prairies.

One of the tangible legacies my maternal grandmother, "The Ange," left was a cookbook in her own hand, which my mother inherited and added to over the years. The pages were filled with the writing of the two women, and a couple of elastic bands were necessary to hold this fat, unruly volume together.

Shortly after Christmas one year, when I was seven and my sister, Moira, was 11, Mother heard us talking in our bedroom, behind the closed door. I had just received a doll and carriage with clothes and linens that would make today's Barbie cry. All satin and lace, done by a very special person in my life, the late Dr. Sigga Houston. Mother heard me saying, "Moira, if there is ever a fire, you have to promise me that you will help me get my doll and carriage out of the house."

Moira replied, "All right, but you have to help me get my new coat out of the house." She had received a new winter coat with real fur on the collar.

Mother whipped open the door and said, "Nonsense. If there is a fire, first we get my cookbook out, and then we go back for your father."

She shut the door, and there was a delayed second before the two of us burst out laughing. We adored our Dad, but that cookbook...

The Jam That Failed

It happened many years ago. Bruno and I were packing to leave for Saskatchewan the following day. However, that afternoon, the first of the local B.C. blueberries appeared at the roadside stands. On impulse, I bought a flat of berries for jam.

I knew the blueberries would be finished before we returned from Saskatchewan, and my annual supply of blueberry jam would be long gone.

Bruno could not believe I was into the jam-making at such a late hour. The rush was on. There was no supply of Certo or small jars on hand, but that seemed trivial. The jam was made and placed in large sealers late that evening.

The rashness of rushing was not apparent until our return. The sealers contained fast-flowing, bright blueberry syrup. I called my friend, Maureen Keith, one of the better cooks around, and a woman of great empathy. She also had three terrific young children, Gillian, Geoffery and Sally, who loved French toast and pancakes. Do you think the kids might like some blueberry syrup, I asked? Oh, I am sure they would, replied my ever-gracious friend.

I felt guilty off-loading the entire supply on her. And I kicked myself again for my initial stupidity.

A year later, Sally, the youngest, age seven by then, asked, "Does Nancy have any more of that Jam That Failed?"

Thus began a tradition. It was no use trying to tell this seven year old that she was ruining my reputation as a cook. Better to keep her quiet with more Jam That Failed.

So part of the blueberry jam-making over the years has been devoted to a separate label, "the Jam That Failed." Bruno became an expert at both, and, like the kids, saved some for his French toast.

THE JAM THAT FAILED

4 cups blueberries, washed

4 cups sugar

1 teaspoon butter

Pinch of salt

2 teaspoons fresh lemon juice

Place berries in a large heavy pot, and crush them with a potato masher, over medium high heat. As soon as the berries begin to bubble, add the sugar, butter and lemon juice, and stir well to keep the berries off the bottom of the pot.

When the berries reach a full boil, a boil that you cannot stir down, allow the boil to continue for approximately 30 seconds, but certainly no longer than one minute, then remove the berries from the heat. Place in sterilized jars and seal.

MAUREEN'S FEISTY JALAPEÑO PEPPER JELLY

On a trip, a small jar of this tucked into our luggage meant Bruno's hankering for a light something to eat with a glass of wine before dinner would be answered. Red wine. Bruno was a dedicated fan. He liked it at "Castle" room temperature. None of that lukewarm, drawing room, 72 degree wine for him.

Place green peppers, jalapeños and Cayenne in a food processor and mix. Then put the contents into a large pot on top of the stove, add the vinegar and sugar, and bring to a boil over medium to high heat. Stir until boiling. Add the Certo and food colouring and boil for five minutes, stirring constantly.

Remove from the heat, and skim off any foam. Place into sterilized jars.

Serve the jelly as an hors d'oeuvre, on top of thin flatbread which has a thin layer of cream cheese.

3 green peppers, seeded and chopped

Two 3-1/2 ounce cans jalapeño peppers, with seeds

1-1/2 cups white vinegar

6-1/2 cups white sugar

1/2 teaspoon Cayenne pepper

6 ounce bottle Certo

Several drops green food colouring

Carvings and Jam

On one of our many trips down the coast of Oregon, Bruno and I stopped to see the Devil's Hole, a spectacular formation where the ocean spouts up through a natural opening in the rocks. We lingered for a picnic lunch and fed the starlings. We wandered across the street to a small shop that featured lapis-blue ceramics in the front, and home-made ice cream in the back.

We sampled the ice cream and took it back across the road to our picnic table. Bruno had that puckish look in his eye, and announced we should set up a similar shop in Gibsons, "Carvings and Jam."

Bruno had a wonderful, filled-with-light carving studio built at Gibsons, which he called "the Short House." It was in the style of Native longhouses, but it was small, hence the name. There were days when Bruno lost track of time, carving. Yellow cedar and red cedar, sensual shapes and movements in wood that came from the serene part of his soul.

Surrounding the Short House were bushes of Saskatoon berries, bigger, fatter cousins to those in Saskatchewan. And they became part of our Jam Factory.

Wine-holder hand carved by Bruno

Bruno entertaining Vancouver Art Gallery members on an excursion to Gibsons.

DESSERTS

Bruno could be tempted by most desserts. He almost never made them, but if they were around, he found them difficult to resist. With all food, however, Bruno was moderate. He ate well, and lightly, and knew that quantity was not the hallmark of good eating.

I am the culprit who loves to make those tempting desserts. But my pleasure comes from the production, not the consumption. Desserts were made for occasions. Day to day, we seldom ate desserts, or even had them on hand, other than lots of fruit. Both Bruno and I seemed to prefer fruits orange in colour: papayas, oranges, cantaloupes, mangoes. So healthy. Although I did catch my loved one drizzling Grand Marnier over sliced oranges on occasion. And he never let on that he knew where I squirreled away my cache of dark chocolate.

These are not desserts for daily devouring. We are talking serious party time here.

LEMON AND ORANGE CREAM OVER STRAWBERRIES

Combine the cream, sugar, egg yolks and zest in a heavy sauce pan over medium heat. Stir constantly with a wooden spoon until the mixture thickens and coats the spoon, approximately 10 minutes. Cool. Cover and refrigerate.

Serve over fresh strawberries.

I accused Bruno of being in love with the Henckels zester and this dessert. He said it wasn't love, but admitted he was "very fond" of them.

Fresh strawberries

2 cups whipping cream

1/4 cup white sugar

3 egg yolks, slightly beaten

Grated zest of 1 lemon and 1 orange

LEMON CHIFFON PIE

Pre-bake a 9 inch pie shell.

3/4 teaspoon plain gelatin
1/4 cup cold water
3 eggs, separated
1/4 teaspoon salt
2 tablespoons fresh lemon juice
Grated rind of 1 lemon
1 cup white sugar

Soak the gelatin in 1/4 cup cold water.

In a double boiler put the egg yolks and the salt and lemon juice, plus the grated lemon rind and the sugar.

Cook, stirring constantly, until thick.

Cool somewhat.

Fold this mixture into the beaten egg whites and the dissolved gelatin.

Pour into the pie shell and refrigerate for a couple of hours. Top with whipped cream seasoned with icing sugar and vanilla when it is ready to serve.

PASTRY

1 cup solid Crisco (1/2 lb.)
1 inch from the end of a pound of butter
1 scant teaspoon salt
3 cups flour
1/2 cup ice water
1 tablespoon white vinegar

Cream together the Crisco and butter. Add the salt. Cream these three ingredients together. Then add the flour, one cup at a time.

Add the vinegar to the ice water, then mix them into the batter.

Wrap the pastry in wax paper and refrigerate.

This should make two covered pies and 1 shell. It will keep in the fridge for about two weeks.

JESSIE'S NORWEGIAN CREAM

In a Pyrex measuring cup, soak the gelatin in 1/4 cup (use a pyrex measuring cup) of cold water for a few minutes. Fill up to the 1 cup line with boiling water, stir until dissolved. Set aside to cool.

Add the lemon juice when cool.

Leave the cup of gelatin in the fridge or a bowl of ice cubes until the liquid begins to move slowly, but before it begins to actually jell.

Separate the eggs and beat the egg whites until they are stiff and form peaks.

Beat the 4 egg yolks and sugar until creamy. Add the cooled gelatin and mix well. Fold in the stiffly beaten egg whites. Place in a large dish, and leave enough room at the top for the strawberry and whipped cream topping. Refrigerate for at least 2 or 3 hours.

When the gelatin has set, spread the strawberry jam and fresh or frozen strawberries on top, and garnish with whipped cream.

This is a very simple dessert, but unless you catch the gelatin at the right stage, it will not work. It means keeping an eye on the gelatin to catch it just as the liquid begins to get slow-moving and a bit thick, but before it actually jells.

Serves 8 to 10 people.

1 envelope plain gelatin

1/4 cup cold water, 3/4 cup boiling water

Juice of 1 lemon

4 eggs, separated

1/2 cup sugar

1/2 cup strawberry jam

1 cup fresh strawberries, sliced*

1 cup seasoned whipping cream (seasoned with vanilla and icing sugar)

*You can substitute thawed frozen strawberries for the fresh berries.

PINEAPPLE DESSERT

1 box of Dad's cookies or 1/2 box graham crumbs

1/2 cup melted butter

1/2 cup of soft butter

1-1/2 cups sugar

2 eggs

1 can crushed, drained pineapple

1/2 pint whipped cream, seasoned with a few
   drops of vanilla and 2 tablespoons icing sugar

Crush the cookies into crumbs, and put 1/2 cup to one side. Combine the remainder with the melted butter, place this first layer in a square glass pan, and put in the oven for 10 minutes at 300 degrees F. Remove from the oven and let cool.

For the second layer, combine the butter and sugar together, beat well, and add the two eggs, beating well. This is the second layer of the dessert.

Combine the pineapple with the whipped cream. The third layer is the combined whipped cream and pineapple.

The fourth and top layer is the remaining 1/2 cup of crumbs from the Dad's cookies. Sprinkle on top with abandon.

Refrigerate for at least four hours or overnight.

Whenever this was in the fridge, spoonfuls of it would mysteriously disappear every time Bruno was near the kitchen.

READ-A-BOOK RUM BANANAS

6 bananas

1 cup whipped cream

4 tablespoons brown sugar

1-1/2 tablespoons rum

Whip the cream until stiff. Add the brown sugar and rum. Mix with thinly sliced bananas and heap into large sherbet glasses.

This dessert guarantees lots of time to keep reading your latest thriller. It's a rich dessert, recommended to follow a light supper.

REAL LEMON SOUFFLÉ

Bruno loved this dish, and was always willing to sit down to grate the rind from the three lemons, a time-consuming prerequisite to making the soufflé.

Talk someone into grating the rind of the lemons. Squeeze the juice from the lemons and set both rind and juice to one side.

Soak the two packages of gelatin in 1/2 cup of cold water. Then dissolve the gelatin over low heat until the liquid becomes clear, but not too hot. Set aside to cool. Do not let the gelatin start to set.

Whip the cream and place in the refrigerator until ready to use.

Separate the eggs, and beat the egg whites until stiff.

Combine the egg yolks and sugar and beat until thick. Add the lemon rind then the juice. Beat until well combined.

Add the whipped cream to this egg-and-sugar mixture, then add the gelatin. Fold in the egg whites and pour into your favourite large dish.

Let the dessert set in the refrigerator for a few hours, or preferably overnight. This is a good recipe to make a day ahead of time.

Before serving, you can dot the soufflé with small rosettes of whipped cream and some shaved Belgian chocolate on top if desired. But it is splendid on its own.

This will usually serve 12 to 15 people.

5 eggs separated

1-1/2 cups sugar

2 cups whipping cream

3 lemons

2 packages unflavoured gelatin

WARTIME CHOCOLATE CAKE

Preheat oven to 375 degrees F and line an 8 x 8" cake tin with wax paper.

1-1/2 squares unsweetened chocolate, melted

2 tablespoons butter

1 cup sugar

1 egg, beaten

1 cup milk, room temperature

1-1/3 cups cake flour, sifted

1 teaspoon baking soda

1/4 teaspoon baking powder

Melt the chocolate in a small Pyrex dish placed in a pan of water over low heat. Do not overcook or burn the chocolate.

Combine the melted chocolate with the butter. Add to this mixture the sugar, then the egg and beat all well. Add the milk alternately with the flour, which has been sifted together with the soda and baking powder. Beat all well.

Place into the cake tin. Bake at 375 degrees F for 30 minutes.

BEST EVER CHOCOLATE ICING

Confession is supposed to be good for the soul. I usually make a double recipe.

1 cup icing sugar

2 tablespoons soft butter

1/4 cup light cream or less

1-1/2 squares unsweetened chocolate, melted

1 egg

1 teaspoon vanilla

Pinch of salt

Melt the chocolate slowly in Pyrex dish over warm water. Let it cool slightly.

Beat together the icing sugar, butter, cream, salt and the egg. Add the chocolate and the vanilla, and beat well with a hand-mixer or in a mix-master until it has the consistency of whipped cream. Do not allow the icing to stay at room temperature for too long or it will melt.

If the icing will not form into the consistency of whipped cream or icing, refrigerate the bowl, beaters and mixture until well chilled, and try beating it again.

The early days at Stratford found Bruno among his professional peers, friends such as Douglas Campbell, Jeremy Wilkin, Christopher Plummer. There was little money – but enormous talent, and fun.

When Bruno cooked in those early days at Stratford, both Douglas Campbell and Jeremy Wilkin recall the huge pot of spaghetti and Bruno's sauce, "a cauldron of spaghetti sauce" for parties of sixty to one hundred people. Bruno became an imperative chef, not only setting up his own barbecue, but actually building it with bricks, a skill learned from his father. Jeremy Wilkin said there was a kind of magic that Bruno brought about with his parties. They had the effect of deflating and defusing any bad feelings that might have arisen amongst the actors in the troupe. The therapy worked on everybody, sharing food, wine and laughter, and one another's company.

One of Bruno's favourite sayings came from those days when Bruno would joke about disgruntled theatre patrons, supposedly throwing tomatoes, cabbages, rotten eggs, whatever – at hapless actors, "Rather large confetti they're throwing tonight."

ANGEL FOOD WITH TOPPING

(Bless Duncan Hines)

Bake a Duncan Hines angel food cake. I keep one in the freezer. Then use whatever toppings you want.

Combine all in a bowl and stir together. Refrigerate for at least 3 or 4 hours.	**Chocolate Whipped Cream Topping**
Remove from the refrigerator and beat with an electric mixer until the consistency of icing.	10 tablespoons white sugar
	6 tablespoons unsweetened cocoa
Cut the Angel Food in half, to create a top and bottom layer, and put a generous amount of the topping in the middle, and the rest of it over the top of the Angel Food.	Pinch of salt
	2 to 3 cups whipping cream
(If it is for a birthday, don't forget to hide the quarters and the loonies in wax paper throughout the middle of the cake.)	3 teaspoons vanilla

JESSIE'S ICE BOX COOKIES

These were Jessie's favourite cookies, and their delicate taste lured even me away from chocolate. Momentarily. Bruno liked anything with nuts or raisins.

1-1/2 cups butter

1 cup brown sugar

1 cup white sugar

3 eggs

4-1/2 cups flour

1 teaspoon cinnamon

1/2 teaspoon salt

1-1/2 teaspoons baking soda

1 cup pecans, chopped

Cream the butter and sugars in the food processor, add the eggs and mix them in well. Put mixture into a large mixing bowl.

Sift together the flour, salt, soda and cinnamon, and stir into the first mixture. Add in the pecans.

Pack tightly into four separate rolls in wax paper and refrigerate for 2 or 3 hours, or overnight.

When ready to bake, preheat the oven to 375 degree F and slice the rolls into thin cookies.

Bake on a greased cookie sheet for about 10 minutes, or until light golden brown.

Chocolate Mousse

LAST MINUTE
CHOCOLATE MOUSSE

*This procedure is thanks to a great chocolate cookbook, **Nuts About Chocolate**, put out in 1983 by Susan Mendelson and Deborah Roitberg, published by Douglas & McIntyre Ltd. Mendelson and Roitberg had a recipe called "Unbelievable Chocolate Mousse," which set out this procedure, using the food processor and the boiling water. Their book is great, and I have used their recipe, with variations, for years, initially using the chocolate chips suggested in their recipe, but later substituting Belgian chocolate.*

Whip the cream together with the vanilla and the icing sugar. Set to one side. Keep in the refrigerator if there is going to be a delay making the rest of the recipe.	1 cup whipping cream
	4 or 5 drops vanilla
Separate the eggs, and beat the egg whites until stiff.	2 tablespoons icing sugar
Put the chocolate into the Cuisinart and mix at high speed for a few seconds. Slowly add the boiling water, then add the egg yolks, one at a time. Continue to process. Then add the vanilla.	2 cups Belgian semi-sweet dark chocolate, chopped or grated
	1/3 cup boiling water
Fold the chocolate mixture into the beaten egg whites. Then fold the whipped cream into that mixture.	4 eggs, separated
The mousse can be served immediately, or can be made a few hours ahead of time.	2 teaspoons vanilla
Top with a small swirl of whipped cream and chocolate shavings to be really wicked.	

TRIPLE THREAT

1 pint vanilla ice cream

6 ounces cognac

2 ounces crème de cacao
   or crème de menthe

Place all in a blender, combine, and serve
in small sherbet glasses.

Be ready for seconds and overnight guests.

We preferred the flavour of the crème de cacao,
but for Christmas and St. Patrick's Day, the
green crème de menthe looks cool.

Triple Threat

A few years ago, Bruno was in Victoria for a day-long cooking demonstration. He was doing several of his favourite recipes, including Umberto's prawns, and honey and orange chicken. One of the desserts he chose was Triple Threat, whose origins are lost in time.

The night before the demonstration, Bruno, staying at a hotel in Victoria, had dinner with friends and then a couple of drinks in the bar. He telephoned before going to sleep, somewhat mellow from his evening of dinner and drinks. "Now tell me again the proportions for the Triple Threat."

So I told him: One brick of vanilla ice cream, six ounces of brandy and two ounces of creme de cacao. It all goes into the blender and makes a very pleasant, somewhat toxic milkshake.

A couple of days later back in Vancouver, Bruno was telling friends at dinner some of the tales from the cooking day demonstration. He laughed and said that some charming and elderly women had been particularly smitten with the Triple Threat. When one of our guests asked him what that was, Bruno explained, "One brick of ice cream, 6 ounces of brandy and 6 ounces of creme de cacao."

"You know," he marvelled, "Some of those women came back for seconds and thirds, and it was in the morning."

JESSIE'S
BOILED
RAISIN CAKE

Preheat oven to 375 degree F and line an 8 x 8" (or smaller) cake tin with wax paper.

1-1/2 cups raisins
1-1/3 cups water
3/4 cup white sugar
1/2 cup butter
2 eggs, separated
1 teaspoon cinnamon
1/4 teaspoon nutmeg
1/8 teaspoon ground cloves
1 teaspoon baking soda dissolved in a little
    warm water
1-1/2 cups flour

Cover the raisins with the 1-1/3 cups of water and simmer for 20 minutes. Strain, save and cool the raisin water.

Beat together the sugar, butter, 2 yolks and 1 egg white.

Add 3/4 cup of raisin water to the butter and sugar mixture. Then add the cinnamon, nutmeg, cloves, and soda until well mixed.

Stir in the flour. Add raisins last.

Pour into the cake tin.

Bake at 375 degrees F for 40 minutes.

Top with seven-minute brown sugar frosting.

SEVEN
MINUTE
FROSTING

3 egg whites
3/4 cup brown sugar
Pinch of salt
6 tablespoons light corn syrup
1 teaspoon vanilla

Put the unbeaten egg whites, sugar, syrup and salt in an upper double boiler over hot water. Beat until the water boils. Then beat for seven minutes, or until the mixture stands in firm mounds. Remove from the heat. Beat in the vanilla. Keep beating until the frosting stands in peaks and holds its shape.

If your cake is in an 8 x 8" pan, reduce the recipe by one third, as these ingredients make a very generous amount of frosting.

Or go wild, and go for the whole amount.

CHOCOLATE LOG

Add water to egg yolks, beat, add sugar, beat, and add vanilla.

Sift the flour and the cocoa together.

Beat the egg whites with the salt added. Fold in the yolk mixture, and fold in the flour mixture.

Bake on a 10 x 14" cookie sheet with raised edges that has been covered with wax paper. Use a moderate oven, 325 degrees F, 12 to 15 minutes.

Remove from the oven and put immediately on a clean piece of wax paper sprinkled with icing sugar. Roll up with the wax paper and let cool.

3 eggs, separated

2 tablespoons water

1/2 cup sugar

3 tablespoons cocoa (unsweetened)

5 tablespoons flour

1 teaspoon vanilla

1/4 teaspoon salt

Filling

In the top of a double boiler put the cold water; sprinkle the teaspoon of plain gelatin over it; let stand for 5 minutes. Dissolve over warm water. Place the whipping cream in a bowl and beat. Add the dissolved gelatin, whip, and add the icing sugar and vanilla. Set in the fridge for 1 hour before putting inside the roll.

If desired, top the log with chocolate icing or hot chocolate sauce.

2 tablespoons cold water

1 teaspoon unflavoured gelatin

1 cup whipping cream

1/4 cup icing sugar

1 teaspoon vanilla

CHOCOLATE CHIP COOKIES

If you are going to use chocolate chips, instead of shaved chunks of Belgian chocolate, avoid the packages that say "chocolate flavoured." Go for the Hershey's, or any other brand that promises "pure" chocolate.

Cream the butter, white sugar and brown sugar until light and fluffy.

Add eggs and vanilla. Beat until smooth.

Sift together the flour, baking soda and salt. Stir into the previous mixture until all the flour is blended in.

Stir in *at least* 2 cups of shaved Belgian chocolate chunks or chocolate chips.

Add more chocolate chunks or chocolate chips if the dough will handle it.

Drop the dough by tablespoon onto ungreased cookie sheets, approximately 2 inches apart.

Bake at 350 to 375 degrees F for 8 to 10 minutes, or until golden.

1 cup butter

1/2 cup white sugar

1 cup firmly packed light brown sugar

2 eggs

2 teaspoons vanilla

2 cups white flour, pre-sifted

1 teaspoon baking soda

1 teaspoon salt

2 cups semi-sweet Belgian chocolate chunks or two cups chocolate chips

P O P C O R N
C R I S P

10 cups popped popcorn

1-1/2 cups mixed nuts

1 cup butter

1-1/3 cups white sugar

1/2 cup Lily white corn syrup

1 teaspoon vanilla

In a heavy pot place the butter, sugar and syrup, stirring all the time until the syrup spins a thread from a spoon or tests on ice water at the hard crack stage. Remove from the heat and add the vanilla; this makes toffee. Pour the toffee over the popcorn and nuts. (The popcorn and nuts should have been kept warm in a large pot in a 275 degree F oven.)

Stir the mixture well to coat the nuts and popcorn with the toffee. Press into two buttered cookie sheets, flatten as thin as possible.

Let harden, break into pieces, and try not to keep it all to yourself.

Bruno's Energy

Bruno had an energy that defied boundaries, and never needed a food source. "He is the only person I know who can grow hair all over his body in 30 seconds," said LaVerne Barnes, a dear friend and fan. Bruno laughed and never denied it.

He had presence that few are born with. Seeing Bruno on stage was unforgettable. I first saw him as Romeo in the 1960 Stratford production of "Romeo and Juliet", and never recovered.

Following Bruno's death, Philip Keatley, who began "The Beachcombers", in which Bruno starred for 19 years as Nick Adonidas, wrote of Bruno's enormous energy in the CBC Staff Publication, "Station Break", "Gerussi was one of the most concentrated balls of energy that ever hit the Mother Corp. (CBC) between the eyes."

And Keatley recalled how Bruno "hit Stratford... like a cyclone." Where the great Tyrone Guthrie told Keatley, "Bruno's presence in a major role pushed the whole Company's energy up twenty percent." Bruno had the same effect in the kitchen.

OCCASIONS

PICNICS

My family were serious picnickers. We never used terms like "nurture" or "bond" in those early days – but you get the picture. Our collection of picnic utensils, coolers and thermos bottles was always on the ready, a tradition I maintain.

Bruno initially was a sceptic. He was appalled at the number of coolers I would hand him to put in the car for trips, long or short. But he really had his own style when it came to picnics. One of his first presents to me, many years ago, was an elaborate wicker picnic basket, containing everything except silver goblets. My sister, Moira, added those.

In 1974, I was in hospital in Toronto for 3-1/2 months, with Bruno juggling "Celebrity Cooks" in Ottawa and the rest of his time in Toronto. Thanks to Bruno, I had the most constant and contented stream of visitors over that period. Bruno set up a bar on the window sill of the Toronto General Hospital, which was apparently invisible to hospital officials, but not to our friends.

When hospital food took its toll, and weight loss became a problem for the first and only time in my life, Bruno began to bring in impromptu picnics, wonderful thin-sliced roast beef, big, fresh prawns, home-baked treats from a favourite bakery. Always done with that artist's eye for presentation. Even in the early days, when they were few and far between, Bruno could scout out the best deli.

To picnic is to love.

CHICKEN HONEY AND ORANGE

1 chicken, cut into pieces for frying
1/4 cup honey
2 oranges, sliced in rounds, unpeeled
1 or 2 tablespoons butter (optional)

Arrange the pieces of chicken on the bottom of a shallow roasting pan. Drizzle honey over them and arrange the orange slices overtop.

Add the butter, if desired.

Place in a 325 degree F oven for approximately an hour, turning the chicken once or twice to make sure it gets coated on both sides.

Great for picnics. Take moist cloths for cleanup of sticky hands.

PICNIC SUGGESTIONS

You can picnic out on your own lawn, with few restrictions. These suggestions assume you have to transport your picnic, so it features food easily packed and stored. You need coolers and ice packs, and thermos jugs for the lemonade or other hot or cold drinks.

I strongly recommend a cooler of ice cubes, to add to the cold drinks like lemonade, and to chill the white wine, or fresh squeezed orange juice, or soft drinks, beer, champagne, or whatever. If you are filling a large cooler with soft drinks and beer, put the drinks in first, with the ice cubes over top. There are some of us who keep a big bag of ice cubes in the freezer, just for such occasions.

- Salami, sliced paper-thin

- Slices of cheddar and gouda cheese, with crackers

- Italian bread and grapes

- Gravlax, sliced thin, with rye or brown bread; and gravlax sauce in a small separate container

- Lemonade

Bruno was probably into the cold beer at this point, and it had been established that I was the designated driver.

- Chicken, done with honey and orange

- Pasta salad, from your favourite deli or home-made.

- Fresh bread or rolls, and butter in a small plastic container. Don't forget a knife for the butter.

- Sliced red, green and yellow peppers, and celery and carrot sticks. These all look great in a plastic bowl or baggies.

You should be sampling the chilled champagne by now.

- Fresh strawberries, washed, but with the green stems left on. A small container of seasoned whipped cream (vanilla and icing sugar), and another small container of demerara sugar. Dip the end of the strawberry first into the whipped cream and then into the sugar. Bruno's idea of heaven.

You will need knives and forks, plates (paper or real ones), napkins, lots, and wet cloths in a plastic bag for clean up. Moira's silver goblets are always on a picnic, because they are large enough, keep the drinks cold, and never break.

The Kitchen

He could have been an architect. Bruno had a feeling for structures and design - and his innovations on our residences over the years always highlighted the kitchen and dining area. Open, expansive, inviting - the heart and centre of the home. No tiny, claustro-phobic galley kitchens for him. The kitchens flowed into the dining areas and made for great entertaining.

No matter how much preparation is done ahead of time, the kitchen requires more than a cameo appearance, once the guests are there. In Bruno's open kitchens, the chef never missed the action; he was the action.

Gibsons

Winter Piano Party

Bruno loved my parents' Saskatchewan winter piano tale, during the early war years, when rationing may have affected the food and liquor supply, but never the spirit. It was a bitterly cold, below-zero New Year's Eve, in those years when women wore long chiffon formals and men were in tuxedos. Pre-dinner festivities were at Mom and Dad's, with dinner at General Ross' home two blocks away. (No, he wasn't dodging WWII, he was a Brigadier General from WWI.)

Mabel Watchler was pounding the ivories on our large upright piano, the sing-song in full cry, when it was time to head up Second Avenue for the other half of the night. But there was no piano at the Ross residence. No problem, said Jessie, we'll bring ours. The livery stable was just a few blocks from our home, so they passed the hat for the $5.00 charge, and the team of horses pulling the large flat-bed dray arrived. The big piano was carried down the steps and loaded on, Mabel resumed playing, the guests piled on, and the travelling carol singers, winter coats over formal gowns, arrived in freezing triumph.

The party was a huge success. When it was time to leave, they woke up the man at the livery stable, passed the hat again, and the piano came home. Our piano tuner, the gentle Mr. Vance, never really forgave Mom and Dad for their brutality to the piano. It took him a year and three tunings to bring it back to life.

Best Guests

We were always blessed with the best guests – the ones who ignored the silly adage – you never discuss politics, religion and sex. Instead, they scorned the two party-killer topics, dieting and money. Guests who have brought the joy of their friendship through our doors and enriched our lives.

As hosts you provide the setting, but it is your friends who make the gathering memorable, who bring their spirit to the occasion.

Every party needs a spark-plug. One couple always brought a radiant presence and their special brand of frisky humour, Tony and Diane Pantages. There were times when Bruno was down, those times we all have when our spirits need lifting. I'd suggest we call Tony and Diane over for dinner, because it was friends like Tony or Alex Pappas or Jackson Davies who never failed to revive Bruno's spirit. In the East it was Grant McLean, Bill Cunningham and others who shared those special bonds.

Diane Pantages continues to energize every room she enters, but she lost our beloved Tony to cancer the year before Bruno died. Lord knows what those two devils are up to in heaven now, because together, they were a wonderful and wicked team, certain insurance against a dull party.

ORANGE SYRUP

8 oranges

8 cups water

8 cups sugar

2 oz. citric acid

Put the oranges through a fine grinder or Cuisinart, then into a large container and add water, sugar, plus 2 ounces of citric acid.

Let stand for 24 hours, then strain. This makes 3 quarts.

For a cool, refreshing, summer drink, put a small amount of syrup and lots of ice in a glass, then fill with water. A thermos of this on your picnic beats those powdered drinks.

To make a Planters Punch rum drink, fill a tall glass with crushed ice. Then fill the glass with a mixture of 1/3 dark rum, 1/3 syrup and 1/3 pineapple juice. Or alternatively, 1/2 rum and 1/2 orange syrup.

Only 2 to a customer. Confiscate the car keys.

Jessie would serve these in the early years with over-proof rum. Until Johnny Logan broke his ribs on the piano bench while leg wrestling on the floor.

JESSIE'S 85TH BIRTHDAY

Jessie celebrating Nancy's 50th birthday at Gibsons.

Part of the fun of a big party is getting the house and surroundings ready. Bruno was getting more and more into gardening. I think he was into a little Zen when he was outside watering, and dead-heading flowers.

Dusting or vacuuming never took our attention as much as making sure the vases were filled with flowers. Once they were, the house was ready for the party, and so were we.

There was one very important party where flowers were forbidden. It was my Mom's 85th birthday, and she had developed an intolerance for flowers, with asthma and emphysema complications. It was Mother, by the way, who used to say she phoned Bruno's number just to hear his recorded messages, because she loved the way he spoke so beautifully. They were old friends, and Bruno read the eulogy when Mom died a year later. She would have loved that.

But what about this party? We had to make it special. Balloons. Many, many balloons. Bruno and I were new to the Balloon School of Decorating at that point. We knew enough to rent an air machine to blow them up, but not enough to buy the little plastic clips that seal the balloon once inflated. So Bruno manually knotted hundreds of balloons after they were inflated. He ended up with a pulverized and bleeding index finger.

It had taken us hours. We were beginning to think we were crazy. But the end result was glorious. The entire house, patio, pathway and stairs to the road were all blooming with huge bouquets of brightly coloured balloons. The party was on the moment you entered the door. Jessie, who had polished party-throwing credentials of her own, was thrilled.

The balloons were such a hit, I almost forgot the food. For Jessie – her favourite – a standing rib roast of beef, cooked medium rare by Bruno, mashed potatoes, creamed onions, and peas, followed by her famous Norwegian cream. Bruno made sure, as always, that we did not forget the roast in the oven and overcook it. And ever the craftsman, he sharpened the carving knives so he could slice the beef thin.

CREAMED ONIONS

When Val and Dave Chapman came for dinner, and there was a roast of beef or roast lamb on the menu, Dave and I were much more delighted than either Bruno or Val to see creamed onions as part of the meal. The addition of fennel to the recipe is an inspired one, thanks to June O'Connor, whose cooking has dazzled us for years. The original recipe did not include the fennel, so we have marked it as optional, in the event that a fennel bulb is not available.

Boil the sliced onions in salted water until they are almost transparent. This does not take long. 2 or 3 minutes before they are cooked, add the sliced fennel. Cook altogether for the last three minutes and drain.

In a heavy sauce pan melt the butter, add the flour and stir until the mixture bubbles. You can also add the sugar, nutmeg, salt and pepper at this time. Add the milk, stirring constantly until the white sauce mixture is smooth and bubbling. This is best over a medium heat, not the highest heat. Once the white sauce has bubbled for a few minutes, remove from the heat and fold in the onion and fennel slices.

This is a good dish to make ahead of time, even one day ahead if you are pressed for time. The dish can be reheated either in the oven at 300 degrees F until it is hot throughout, or in the microwave. To let the flavours blend with the sauce, I prefer leaving it in a 300 degrees F oven for about one-half hour before serving.

1 large onion, chopped, fairly large slices

1 fennel bulb, sliced down the bulb and julienned (optional)

2 tablespoons butter

2 tablespoons flour

Pinch of white sugar

Pinch of nutmeg

Salt and ground pepper to taste

3/4 cup milk

OVERNIGHT BAKED HAM

1 large "cooked" ham
1/2 cup brown sugar
6 tablespoons dry mustard
355 mL (12 oz.) can ginger ale
1/3 cup cloves

Place the ham in a large roasting pan. Score the fat with diagonal crossed knife slashes, and insert at each intersection of the scoring 1 or more cloves. Add additional cloves to the bottom of the pan for flavour.

Then pour over the ham a mixture of the ginger ale, brown sugar and dry mustard. Place in the oven uncovered for approximately 1 hour at 300 degrees F. Cover with heavy tinfoil, but not so tightly that the air does not vent. Leave in the oven overnight at 250 or 275 degrees F. Alternatively, cook throughout the day, uncovered, and keep basting, if you have the time. You can cook at a higher temperature if your time is limited, but slower cooking gives the best results. 10 hours at low heat is not too much for an 18 pound ham.

You will know the ham is done when it appears to come away from the end of the bone, and it should be cooked evenly. If the top is not brown enough before serving, turn up the heat for a short time, and baste a couple of times.

Jackson's Meats on West 4th Avenue in Vancouver has provided the best hams for three generations, curing them with special wizardry.

JACQUIE'S HAM SAUCE

1/3 cup butter
1 cup brown sugar
2 teaspoons curry
1 - 14 ounce can peaches
1 - 14 ounce can pears
1 - 14 ounce can apricots
3 - 7 ounce cans mandarin sections
1/2 cup raisins
1/2 cup almonds
1/4 cup maraschino cherries

Melt the butter and add the brown sugar and curry.

Drain the peaches, pears and apricots. Cut the fruit into bite size pieces.

Combine everything into an oven proof dish, mixing the melted butter, sugar and curry well into the mixture.

Cook uncovered in the oven for 1 hour at 325 degrees F.

Can be served hot or cold with the ham (which can also be served hot or cold).

You can substitute any fresh or tinned fruit you have on hand. Everything seems to work.

Bruno was someone who took care of others. He was generous to a fault. As a host, he was wonderful. Although you had to be prepared to defend your political and social arguments, sometimes in a loud voice. And there were times when it was tough to shout over those Shakespearean tonsils that were known to bellow, "Bullshit!" in moments of political passion.

Overnight Baked Ham

DON'T TELL CHICKEN DRUMETTES

We have served this mainly as an hors d'oeuvre, but friends do this as a main course with chicken thighs, and add garlic to season before cooking.

Don't tell anyone how easy this is.

1-1/2 lbs. of chicken drumettes

2/3 cup oyster sauce

1/3 cup plum sauce

Cover the bottom of a shallow baking pan with the drumettes.

Pour oyster sauce liberally overtop of the drumettes.

Then put the plum sauce over the drumettes and oyster sauce.

Place uncovered in the oven at 325 degrees F for at least 1 hour. Or at 275 degrees F for 2 hours, depending on your time frame. Turn them over once or twice.

Shirley Spafford introduced us to this use of oyster sauce years ago, one Saskatchewan evening at the lake.

MOIRA'S GO SKATING FLANK STEAK

My late sister, Moira, could out-barbecue even Bruno. Unlike k.d., she had a Calgarian's passion for beef. If the snow were too deep for the barbecue, and you could keep her huge black cat, Sam, from spearing the olives out of your martini, this flank steak was sure to follow.

Score the steak by knife cuts diagonally across the meat.

Mix all but the flank steak together well, and place the mixture over the flank steak. Then roll the steak loosely, and tie it at several places with string.

Place the rolled steak onto a lightly oiled piece of heavy tinfoil and fold and secure the foil around it, but leave enough room inside for juices to bubble up.

Cook the steak in a 200 degree F oven for 4 to 5 hours. Then, for the last 1/2 hour, open up the foil, and cook the steak in a hotter oven for that last 1/2 hour to brown it.

1 flank steak

1/2 cup bread crumbs

1 small garlic clove, chopped

2 tablespoons onion, chopped fine

2 tablespoons celery, chopped fine

A pinch of cayenne pepper

1 teaspoon parsley

1 teaspoon basil

1/8 teaspoon dry mustard

1 egg, slightly beaten

Salt and pepper to taste

S P A R E R I B S

The Big 5-0

Our friend, Gary Lauk, was about to do the unforgivable – let his 50th birthday pass without a murmur. He was refusing to let us throw a party at our place for him, or to have one himself. Bruno and I finally prevailed, and at our insistence, we catered the party – at Gary's home, inviting some of his favourite people. Bruno ruled the kitchen that night, sang in Italian, cooked and entertained, and the guests refused to stay out of Gary's spacious kitchen, which is where all the best parties happen anyway. Now, Lauk pretends he is turning 50 every year.

Brown the ribs in a shallow pan in a 450 degree F oven. Then place in an ovenproof dish with the brown sugar, water and the soya and plum sauce.

Cook in a 350 degree F oven for approximately 1 hour.

Make a sauce from the vinegar and brown sugar, with ketchup to thicken. Add the squeeze of lemon juice, garlic, and salt and pepper. Combine and pour over the ribs and cook for about 30 minutes in the oven before serving.

Spareribs

3/4 cup brown sugar
3/4 cup water
3 tablespoons soya sauce
3 tablespoons plum sauce

Sauce

1/4 cup vinegar
1/2 cup brown sugar
Ketchup to thicken, approximately
   1/3 cup
Squeeze of fresh lemon juice
Garlic clove, crushed (optional)
Salt and pepper to taste

ROAST LAMB

"The Beachcombers" goes to Greece.

Top: Nancy and Jackson Davies

Bottom: Bruno recharging his photo-voltaic cells in the Mediterranean

We both shared an appetite for lamb, in any form. And often when dining out, lamb would be our choice, whether it was in one of Umberto's restaurants, a French restaurant, or a Greek restaurant. Vancouver boasts our famous Salt Spring Island lamb.

When they decided to film an episode of "The Beachcombers" in Greece several years ago, we anticipated the same delicious lamb that we had always had in Greek restaurants in Vancouver and Toronto. It was not to be.

The three weeks in Greece were heavenly. We loved the people; the country, climate, history and architecture all exceeded our expectations. But we seemed to hit one dismal meal after another. Jackson and Linda Davies were with us for most of the time, and we all found ourselves playing safe with daily Greek salads, trying to avoid meals smothered in excess olive oil. Jackson referred to it as "three weeks of bobbing for olives."

To be fair, we did have some good meals, but not one of lamb. Our most wonderful meal in Greece was our last night there, with Greece's leading actors, generous and wonderful hosts, who took us to a rooftop restaurant late on a warm August evening, looking directly over to a flood-lit and ultimately moon-lit Parthenon. It was a scene of wonderment. We were discouraged from ordering the lamb, and our hosts insisted we try the goat instead. It was outstanding. We vowed to return to Greece, but never made it back.

SALT SPRING ROAST LAMB

Lunch at Hastings House, Salt Spring Island, with Tracey and Bill Rand.

Bruno preferred his lamb medium, and I preferred it slightly more done. If the meat has started to come away from the bone, then that indicated to me it was well done. Roasted at 20 minutes per pound in 350 degree Fahrenheit oven should bring it to medium that Bruno preferred.

For "au jus," pour a small amount of the vegetable water into the roasting pan after the meat and vegetables have been removed. Place the pan on high heat on top of the stove, scraping the brown end bits from the pan, and letting the liquid reduce by boiling it.

Cut two garlic cloves into slivers, make small slashes in the roast and insert the slivers of garlic throughout the top. Place the roast in a roasting pan and the remaining two garlic cloves and four onion quarters in the pan. Pour the olive oil over the roast and onion and place the rosemary over the top of the roast. Salt and pepper to taste.

After the roast has been in the oven for about 3/4 hour, boil the potatoes for about 10 minutes in slightly salted water, and the carrots for about 5 minutes in salted water; drain and keep the water, and place the potatoes and the carrots around the roast in the pan.

Baste the roast and the vegetables from time to time with the pan drippings, until the roast is done to your liking.

One of Bruno's many ways of cooking lamb:

Preheat oven to 350 degrees F.

1 leg of lamb, bone in
1 large onion, sliced in quarters
4 or 5 garlic cloves
4 tablespoons olive oil
Salt and pepper to taste
Several sprigs of fresh rosemary (dried rosemary can be substituted)
6 potatoes, peeled and halved, in cold water
12 large carrots, peeled, in cold water

MAUREEN'S EASTERN PATÉ

1 lb. of chicken livers

1-1/2 teaspoons salt

1/8 teaspoon Cayenne pepper

1 cup soft butter

1/2 teaspoon nutmeg

2 teaspoons dry mustard

1/4 teaspoon ground cloves

4 tablespoons of onion

2 tablespoons of sherry or cognac

Place the chicken livers in water, bring to boil, then simmer for 15 to 20 minutes, drain and cool.

Place the cooled chicken livers plus all the rest of the ingredients in the Cuisinart and mix well.

Place in paté serving dishes and chill.

Serve with Melba toast, or crackers, or French bread.

"He was the least dull man I ever knew."

Vicki Gabereau

Surprise

He never saw it coming. Not until the float plane landed out in the ocean for him.

It was May 7th, Bruno's 48th birthday, and he had a full day of filming "Beachcombers" out on a barge somewhere in Howe Sound. I had phoned to wish him happy birthday first thing in the morning from Deep Cove, and the crew had the big birthday cake on hand. He assumed that was pretty well it.

Surprise parties are easy to execute when the target is elsewhere. Bruno had been up at Gibsons for most of the week, so I invited all our friends, and cooked up a storm while he was gone. It was no problem persuading the director to have Bruno's filming finished by 5:00 p.m., hire a float plane to pick up fellow conspirator, Bruce Gorman, first at Gibsons, and then to the barge to carry away Bruno.

Bruce had ensured Bruno's party threads, and a thermos of cold vodka martinis with two glasses were on board. The plane flew Bruno and Bruce to the dock at Deep Cove in North

Vancouver, just a block from my cottage and the scene of the crime. Tony Pantages drove to the dock to pick them up in his vintage red convertible.

The sun was shining on the mountains, the azaleas and rhododendrons were in full bloom, the sea was calm, and the party rocked. I forget how many guests. There was baked ham, and chicken tarragon, one of Bruno's favourite dishes. Inevitably, Maureen's paté, and big trays of fresh cut raw vegetables and cheeses before dinner and a tray of fresh fruit after, along with something more sinful in the form of a birthday cake. I remember giving Bruno a router, before I even quite knew what it was. Bruno always liked tools, and Dave Chapman, whose workshop Bruno coveted, assured me the router would be a success. It was.

Late at night, when the party was over, and the guests were gone, I looked over, and Bruno had tears in his eyes.

And he always teased that I cried at card tricks.

Bruno. A quiet moment in the beauty of Deep Cove.

Bruno and Vicki Gabereau at Bruno's log home in Gibsons.

NEW YEAR'S EVE

Like my Cape Breton Highland father, I always felt New Year's Eve was the most special of nights. Bruno may not have shared the Celtic mysticism about New Year's, but he and I were seldom apart that night and we welcomed the opportunity to have special friends in for New Year's Eve supper. Our favourite combination was fresh Dungeness crab in the shell, grapefruit and poppyseed salad, and French bread, followed by hot dark chocolate soufflé with hot chocolate sauce.

Photo:

*Fresh cracked dungeness crab
at Deep Cove, New Year's.
Alex Pappas, Mimi McIntyre, Bruno*

GRAPEFRUIT & AVOCADO SALAD

Judy LaMarsh introduced us to this salad, and the recipe for poppyseed dressing was also hers.

1 head of lettuce
1-1/2 cups fresh grapefruit sections, drained
1 avocado, peeled and sliced

JUDY'S POPPYSEED DRESSING

1/3 cup fresh lemon juice
1/3 cup fresh orange juice
1 cup olive oil
1/2 cup sugar
1 teaspoon salt
1 teaspoon dry mustard
1 teaspoon grated onion
1-1/2 teaspoons of poppyseeds

Place all but the lettuce, grapefruit and avocado in a jar and shake until blended.

Dip the avocado slices in lemon juice to prevent discolouring.

Arrange the lettuce, with the grapefruit and avocado on top, and serve with poppyseed dressing.

There are also commercial poppyseed dressings, but they tend to be more oil or cream based.

Bruno loved salads. His favourite was a simple combination of butter lettuce and radicchio, featuring its crimson and white leaves, and an oil and vinegar dressing, or simply oil and vinegar, 3 parts oil to 1 part vinegar.

HOT DARK CHOCOLATE SOUFFLÉ
With Belgian Hot Chocolate Sauce

Make the first part of this soufflé, the sauce, in advance and chill. To do this, melt the butter, blend in the flour, let it bubble and cook for a minute or two, stir in the milk, sugar, and chocolate, stir and cook over medium heat until thick and smooth. Cool a little. Stir in the egg yolks until blended, cover and chill in the fridge.

Remove from the fridge 1 hour before serving and stir in the cold water and the vanilla.

Pre-heat oven to 350 degrees F.

Beat the egg whites until stiff, and fold them into the chocolate mixture until smooth. Cook in either 6 individual unbuttered glass or pottery dishes or 1 large unbuttered soufflé dish. Cook by setting in a pan with enough hot water underneath to come halfway up the sides of the dishes. Cook for 40 to 45 minutes in a 350 degree F oven.

Bring out of the oven, dust with icing sugar, and serve immediately with seasoned whipped cream and hot chocolate sauce.

Instructions for Sauce

Combine the chocolate, sugar and cold water in a saucepan. Cook over low heat, stirring occasionally. It will take 15 to 20 minutes. Stir in vanilla just before serving. Yields approximately 2 cups.

Alternatively, use 6 ounces of Belgian semi-sweet chocolate, grated, plus the cold water and the vanilla.

Serves 6.

1-1/2 tablespoon butter

1 tablespoon flour

1/2 cup milk

3/4 cup sugar

2 squares (2 ounces) unsweetened chocolate, melted

4 eggs, separated

1 tablespoon cold water

1/2 teaspoon vanilla

Belgian Hot Chocolate Sauce

3 ounces unsweetened Baker's chocolate, grated

2 tablespoons white sugar

1-1/2 cups cold water

1 teaspoon vanilla

THE DUCK AND THE NAZI

Bruno and Birthday boy Lauk

Bruno carving with his prized, custom hand-made Schoenfeld carving set

Sometimes we would run into Nazis. Not often, but enough to bring out another of Bruno's favourite sayings, "Put a cap and a uniform on a parking lot attendant, and he thinks he's Hitler."

Bruno had a passionate dislike for bullies, and a contempt for those who abused their authority, at whatever level they might happen to be.

The self-important Nazi might be a haughty waitress or the person loading cars onto the ferry. It is a gender-neutral category.

Many years ago, we encountered an unpleasant maître d' at the Camino Real Hotel in Mexico City. It was New Year's Eve, and we had debated going to the very fancy and expensive restaurant in the Hotel, modelled after a famous Parisian one. We both ordered duck as a main course, and our waiter arrived to "carve" the duck at our table, to place on our individual plates. The duck was so tough he literally could not cut into it or sever any portions.

His difficulty became obvious, and the imperious maître d' flounced over and took the carving knife and fork from the hands of the waiter, and banished him. He then

93

proceeded to show how it should be done. Except he couldn't cut the duck either.

We sat transfixed, watching the maître d' become redder and more furious, while we were intimidated, but desperately trying not to laugh out loud. He finally hacked and literally tore the duck apart with his hands, slapped it onto our plates and walked away.

We were overwhelmed with laughter. Bruno began to muse warmly about our duck, about the venerable age he must have reached, and the many thousands and thousands of miles he must have flown, probably from the Arctic, to develop such firm muscles. Needless to say, we couldn't cut into the duck to eat it, and the more we tried, the more we laughed, and the more ingenious Bruno's history of our now-beloved duck became.

After dinner, we repaired to the cocktail lounge adjacent, to fill ourselves up with brandy Alexanders. The maître d' had not come near us, but the rest of the staff must have been aware, because we were treated to a number of drinks by the staff in the bar, and I recall it as one of our more charming New Year's Eve celebrations.

That was December, 1973, and ever since, whenever one of us would order duck, the laughter would return. To my recollection, we never cooked duck.

BRANDY ALEXANDER

Forget the duck. Here is the recipe for Brandy Alexanders.

This is for four drinks.

3 oz. creme de cacao

4 oz. brandy

3 oz. heavy cream

Pinch of nutmeg

Shake all with cracked ice, strain and serve in small martini glass.

Put a dash of nutmeg on top.

Try not to tangle with the maître d'.

New Year's Eve

Scottish tradition demands that the first man to cross the threshold after the stroke of midnight on New Year's Eve must be dark-haired and carry a piece of coal, or failing that, a loaf of bread. If the first who tries to cross your threshold is blond, you are not to let him in or you'll suffer bad luck for a year.

Douglas Campbell, that great Shakespearean actor and director, and life-long friend of Bruno's, was – and no doubt still is – a true Scot. In the 12 years that Bruno and his late wife, Ida, were at Stratford, Dougie always wanted to make sure that it was Bruno, the dark-haired friend, who crossed the Campbell doorstep first.

For Bruno and I, New Year's Eve was a time for a bottle of good champagne (my choice) and some fine brandy (Bruno's choice). If we were in Vancouver, the sound of the ships blowing their horns at midnight ushered in the New Year.

New Year's was a time when Bruno could park his demons for awhile, and he had them. He rode the edge sometimes because he had to, and sometimes because he wanted to. He never wanted to get too comfortable, or too complacent.

This past New Year's Eve, it seemed important to be home in time to hear the ships at the stroke of midnight, and remember the Bruno I knew – the dark-haired stranger who became my best friend, my lover, my mate, my anchor, the person with whom I felt safe and loved and special.

Love and Laughter

Bruno's death left me with profound sadness and despair. All energy was gone. A friend, whose treasured son had died, said, "Your concentration has gone, I know. It takes time to return." He spoke wisdom.

I made the decision to complete this book and gradually the joy of cooking returned to me. The recipes were like old friends, comfortable, undemanding, uncomplicated, sustaining. I began to make dishes once loved, some long ignored, and memories flooded in of Bruno and me in the kitchen, with friends and family, dining out, entertaining in, travelling. With tears and laughter I spread 24 years of photo albums and snapshots all over the house, chronicling great times we had shared, how lucky we were.

And back they came, those twins of production that had deserted me – energy and concentration. It was possible to begin again with such a happy project. Production eventually flowed back into my professional life as well.

Bruno loved my family, as he did his own, and we had wanted our book to intersperse memorable family laughs among the recipes like sticky taffy. The laughter has been an unexpected bonus helping to overcome much of the sadness.

Love and laughter heal. This book has been one of Bruno's final gifts to me, and mine to him.

Acknowledgements

The first thanks should go to all those friends over the years who have kept coming back for more, never minding the last-minute invitations, when the urge to cook suddenly came upon Bruno and me.

My deep gratitude to the tasters and testers of these recipes who picked up more errors than I care to divulge – dear friends who can cook circles around anybody: June O'Connor, who does this for a living and yanked me back from more than one abyss; Jacquie and David Sims, who valiantly tested many of the Saskatchewan recipes which Jacquie remembers from our childhood together, and Leslie, Bill and Rob Sims, their children, who shared in the testing and the laughter; Maureen Keith, for all the testing and recipes, and Sally Keith, for inspiration many years ago and testing today; Judge Dolores Holmes, my other Italian expert; Lana Underhill, who not only tested, but started me on the gravlax many years ago; Dr. Donald Stephens, Professor Emeritus of English at the University of British Columbia, who read the first manuscript and made valuable corrections and suggestions; then he and Dor-Lu, his wife, kitchen enthusiasts both, sampled and critiqued the recipes as well.

Bruno's children, Rico Gerussi and Tina Gerussi, not only encouraged me, but contributed personally to the book, as did Gino Gerussi, Bruno's favourite golfing nephew. And they know I had to censor some of the stories and the language for this book.

To the many friends whose words and love have helped to form this book: Gary Dunford, whose soul touched Bruno's always; Umberto Menghi, who shared himself and his family with us; Vicki Gabereau and Allan Fotheringham, who knew Bruno was one of their biggest fans; Jeremy Wilkin, Douglas Campbell, Diana Filer, Grant and Betty Mclean, Alex Pappas, Jackson Davies, Robert Clothier ("Relic"), Bruce Gorman,

Philip Keatley, professional colleagues who became dear friends and family; to close friends Lauris Talmey, Mike Ryan, LaVerne Barnes, Lisa Hobbs Birnie, Sandra and Hugh Lyons, Alison McLennan, Shirley Spafford, Mary Lou and Bill Swope, Gary Lauk, Theresa and Ed Odishaw, Pattee Flett. And to the precise Jack Webster, who helped check my LaMarsh and Scottish facts, Brian Jackson of Jackson's Meats, Peter Weiser, Dan MacDonald, Madeleine Shaw, Gary Lewchuk, Sheila (Graham) Yeomans, Susan Mendelson, Deborah Roitberg, Duff Waddell, Stuart Clyne, and Margareta.

My thanks to my secretary, Lorraine Kehler, who not only typed the many revised versions of this, but tested some of the recipes as well. And to Patralyn Stanger, who also typed and typed. This book would not exist but for the kinds words of Scott McIntyre and the warm encouragement of my fearless publisher, Pam McColl. It's been a ride. My love and thanks to you all.

RECIPE INDEX

SEVEN MINUTE FROSTING 69
SHEILA'S SEAFOOD CASSEROLE 18
Shellfish *see Seafood*
Soufflé
    Cheese Soufflé with Love 44
    Hot Dark Chocolate Soufflé 92
    Real Lemon Soufflé 66
Soup
    Cape Breton Fish Chowder 18
    Chicken Soup 42
    Chilled Tomato Soup 37
    Easy Corn Chowder 33
Sour Cream
    Veal Cutlets in Sour Cream 30
SPARERIBS 86
Stuffing
    Chicken and Turkey Stuffing 40
Strawberry
    Jessie's Norwegian Cream 64
    Lemon and Orange Cream Over Strawberries 62
    Strawberry Jam 55
STRAWBERRY JAM 55
SUMMER FRUIT BUTTER 52
SWEET PEPPER CRAB CAKES 17
Sweet Potato *see Potato*
TENDER DANDELION GREENS 34
THERESA'S BREAD 51
Tomato
    Chilled Tomato Soup 37
Turkey
    Chicken or Turkey Stuffing 40
    Roast Turkey 41
TRIPLE THREAT 71
UMBERTO'S PRAWNS 16
VEAL CUTLETS IN SOUR CREAM 30
Vegetable
    Bruno's Whistler Carrots 35
    Candied Sweet Potatoes 38
    Cheese Lover's Potatoes 38
    Chilled Tomato Soup 37
    Cooked Salad Dressing 36
    Creamed Onions 82
    Easy Corn Chowder 33
    Grapefruit and Avocado Salad 91
    Madeleine's Stuffed Mushrooms 39
    Pickled Beets 34
    Tender Dandelion Greens 34
WARTIME CHOCOLATE CAKE 67
WILD BLUEBERRY JAM 56